Working with Parents

Working with Parents

A Guide for Education Professionals

Carmel Digman and Sue Soan

Los Angeles • London • New Delhi • Singapore • Washington DC

First published 2008

SAGE Publications Ltd
1 Oliver's Yard
55 City Road
London EC1Y 1SP

SAGE Publications Inc.
2455 Teller Road
Thousand Oaks, California 91320

SAGE Publications India Pvt Ltd
B 1/I 1 Mohan Cooperative Industrial Area
Mathura Road
New Delhi 110 044

SAGE Publications Asia-Pacific Pte Ltd
33 Pekin Street #02-01
Far East Square
Singapore 048763

Library of Congress Control Number: 2007937124

British Library Cataloguing in Publication data

A catalogue record for this book is available from the British Library

ISBN 978-1-4129-4758-9
ISBN 978-1-4129-4759-6 (pbk)

Typeset by C&M Digitals (P) Ltd., Chennai, India
Printed in Great Britain the Cromwell Press, Trowbridge, Wiltshire
Printed on paper from sustainable resources

Contents

Acknowledgements

Clearly, the main acknowledgements for this book have to go to all the home/ school workers who are developing this job into a valuable professional role. When considering the Every Child Matters agenda, professionals such as the home/school workers are enabling many of its aims and objectives to be successfully achieved, frequently being the main link between various statutory authorities and families. For education, the home/school worker's role is particularly significant, because by supporting the families outside of school, the children experiencing difficulties are frequently then able to focus on achieving their best at school, both academically and socially.

We would also like to offer our thanks to Wendy Mann, Sue Dinsdale and other practising home/school workers, for their support and encouragement. Our thanks must also go to the schools from which the case studies have been sourced, but which cannot be named in order to maintain confidentiality. All the case studies are based on compilations of histories going back several years and not on any individual child or family. No original names or places have been used in order to maintain anonymity. Finally, we would like to thank our families for their encouragement and patience.

About the Authors

Carmel Digman BSc (Hons) has been a home/school support worker in primary schools for seven years. She has training in solution focus therapy, social, emotional and behavioural difficulties and multi-agency working. She has experience in a wide range of schools and local areas among communities with diverse needs. As a Senior Family Liaison Officer, she provides guidance, training and supervision to other home/school support workers. She has a degree in psychology and many years' experience working with families in the public, voluntary and private sectors. She has written material for training and for use with children and families devising programmes for bereavement, anger management and social skills. She has worked for 15 years as a catechist with children from age seven to 16. She has five children of her own and is also an illustrator and watercolourist.

Sue Soan is a principal lecturer for the Centre for Enabling Learning, Institutional Development and Inclusion at Canterbury Christ Church University. She is also the Lead Academic for the South East Gifted and Talented Excellence Hub. Prior to this, Sue worked in both mainstream and special educational settings, first as a classroom teacher, then as a subject coordinator and, for over a decade, as a SENCO. It is during her time as a SENCO that she worked with a family liaison worker (FLO), the first in the local authority, and she recognized the potential this role could offer both families and schools. Sue is particularly interested in the areas of motor control development, speech and language, and social, emotional and behavioural needs. She is author and editor of a number of books on special educational needs and inclusion.

Preface

The main purpose of this book is to provide home/school workers with information, reassurance and training in a very accessible format and positive manner. It is not intended that the reader should read the book all at one time, but should utilize the appropriate chapters as applicable to practice situations. The chapters are designed to address topics highlighted in the Every Child Matters (ECM) agenda, heading by heading, evaluating the impact of problems on children's well-being and the ways in which help might be accessed through school. Most of the chapters have case studies which will clearly illustrate points being discussed and explained. Chapters also contain guidelines and suggestions for good practice which can be modified to suit the unique needs of the reader's own school community. Points for reflection and further reading references are provided for each chapter. A number of protocols and proformas are included within the appendices and these can be freely photocopied by readers.

The first chapter considers the role of home/school workers and the extent of the work they undertake. Subsequent chapters are concerned with specific issues facing children and families that impact on their well-being and educational achievement. Not all the issues a home/school support worker may encounter will be found within this short volume, but it is hoped that the ones which are will help you develop and enhance transferable strategies and ideas. The final chapter looks at the future of the role, its potential for dealing with children's educational problems, and the issues it raises for training, safety, supervision and career development.

Finally, the authors hope this book will encourage debate and discussion at many levels. It is envisaged that tutors and teacher trainers will be able to use the case studies and the practical ideas and reflective questions for professional training. Local authorities, clusters of schools and individual institutions similarly should see the value of using such experience and knowledge for practice and training purposes. Also, of course, it is hoped that the expertise and professionalism of home/school workers is positively portrayed throughout this book. It may engender discussion about the need for a specific qualification, and hence professional recognition for this group of workers, who manage to facilitate the crossing of agency and professional boundaries, to enable families to access the appropriate help their children need to achieve.

1

Working with Parents

This opening chapter will focus on identifying the roles and responsibilities of a home/school worker within the context of the 'Every Child Matters' (DfES, 2004) agenda of:

- being healthy
- staying safe
- enjoying and achieving
- making a positive contribution.
- achieving economic well-being

It is firstly important to consider why the initial Green Paper entitled 'Every Child Matters' (ECM) (DfES, 2003) was written and what it hoped to achieve. It was written as a response to the tragic death of Victoria Climbie, and the subsequent inquiry led by Lord Laming, which tried to identify how her death had been allowed to happen and how another such death could be avoided. The government wanted to try to ensure that such a tragedy should never happen again because of the lack of statutory agency action and collaboration. As the then Prime Minister Tony Blair stated:

> we are proposing here a range of measures to reform and improve children's care – crucially, for the first time ever requiring local authorities to bring together in one place under one person services for children, and at the same time suggesting real changes in the way those we ask to do this work carrry out their tasks on our and our children's behalf. (DfES, 2003: 1)

The specific areas of intervention with parents that home/support workers can engage with will also be defined in this chapter. It is seen as a role undertaken by designated school staff members, and therefore the interventions and strategies suggested here will enable these professionals to support children to fully engage with school and their education. The personal safety, the mental and physical health, and general well-being of the home/school support workers will be considered as these are always vital factors to consider when planning interventions.

Understanding the home/school support role in schools requires a clear analysis of the different areas in which the role functions and the impact of the role on children's education. Local authorities and individual schools are increasingly viewing the role as a significant tool to promote closer, positive relationships between school and home, especially encouraging parents to become more involved in the education of their children.

Whether the school designates a specific person to this role or sees it as the shared responsibility of a staff team, home/school liaison aims to develop relationships with families, making 'school' a focal point in the community where the families can access support and advice. The government hope that as daily week-day attendance at school is a statutory requirement, the development of such a role, which is in line with the Every Child Matters agenda, will improve the outcomes for children. Even the most isolated and disaffected families usually make contact with a school. If such families can be encouraged to collaborate in the education of their children, they may be enabled to make positive changes in their lives with help accessed through their home/school support worker.

Where problems are entrenched within a family, interventions offered by other agencies may be time-limited, providing only brief respite and help. However, home/school support offers intervention for as long as the children are in the school and will not immediately withdraw support when improvements are achieved. The authors have found through their experience that over time parents will become confident in approaching school to access help, and when this happens help can be tailored to their long-term, as well as immediate, needs.

Every Child Matters

Being safe
Risks to the safety of children fall within a very broad range of definitions, and school staff, because of their regular contact with children, are more likely to be aware of those 'at risk' children. Risk factors fall into two broad categories:

1 **Environmental risks**: where children are exposed to danger within their environment. Examples are: poor housing and hygiene, domestic violence, bullying, local community violence.
2 **Behavioural risks**: where children are choosing dangerous behaviours. Examples include: substance abuse, dangerous games, criminal activities.

Identification
In the initial stages of any induction into the post as a home/school support worker, families will come to your attention that have a history of concerns and difficulties. Referrals for these children will come from both teaching and support staff, or from parents themselves. Children may also come for advice and may disclose issues that help to identify them as 'at risk'. The referral process is discussed in the 'Points for practice' below. For referrers, identifying features may be:

• parental concerns about peer pressure, bullying, etc.
• children with frequent injuries, however minor

- sustained and reliable reports of risk-taking behaviours or dangerous family circumstances
- outside agency involvement, e.g. police or social services.

While some children will be living lifestyles that involve considerable risks to their safety, others will be exposed to risk because of temporary situations and interventions may only need to be brief.

There are families who are transient for many reasons, such as travellers, families escaping domestic violence, families with housing crises, families avoiding debt repayment, and refugee and immigrant families. Many of these may be facing considerable risks to safety and require help to improve their living conditions.

Interventions

Offering help to families within school will depend upon resources and community links. Part of the development of the role is to 'network' and 'access local resources' from statutory and non-statutory agencies, and voluntary groups. Help should be realistic and accessible and where there is resistance, it should be left open to parents to change their mind. If help is freely offered with clear information about confidentiality and also whom it will involve, then families can make informed choices. (Note: Where children are at risk in any way, then schools' child protection procedures should be followed and referrals may be necessary in the best interest of the child, even if the parents object.)

Interventions are limited only by the imagination and resources of the school and might include:

- simply listening
- giving advice on parenting
- giving advice on debt, housing, addiction, domestic violence
- monitoring children in school and offering individual or group work
- making referrals to other agencies, e.g. Social Services.

Engaging with parents

The school environment is particularly suited to the process of engaging with others on a social level. For most parents, nursery and primary school greatly enlarges their circle of friends and acquaintances. Children make friends and parents follow suit at the school gate and at school events and gatherings. A home/school worker uses these situations and enhances them, introducing parents to wider possibilities including links with services, local knowledge, support in times of difficulty and opportunities to become more involved in the school community. The process may take time and involve considerable effort, particularly if the role and/or the home/school worker are unfamiliar.

Methods used to engage with the families may include any of the following:

- informal chats at the school gate
- appointments made specifically about a given problem
- visiting the family home
- encouraging a parent to help in school in some way

- offering training courses or parent groups
- signposting to specific agencies where appropriate
- accompanying a parent to a meeting
- helping out in a family emergency.

The role may be seen as creating a bridge between families and school and other supporting agencies to overcome disadvantages of education, social confidence and poverty. In this role, you may be seen as the first person a parent/carer may approach when problems occur and the only one available at an easily accessible and non-threatening point, i.e. the school. This makes the role vital because crossing that bridge, or not, may make or break a family. Making the support offered realistic, genuinely relevant, non-judgemental and impartial becomes crucial, if the family is to be engaged and encouraged to move on.

 Case study: Leigh, aged 13

Leigh is 13 and has lived through considerable turmoil with domestic violence, homelessness and bereavement already part of her experience. She is currently refusing to attend school, is drinking heavily and mixing with much older children. Leigh's mother, Sara, has two younger children and works part-time. She is finding Leigh increasingly difficult to handle.

Agencies involved with Leigh have included the local community police, Educational Welfare and Attendance Officers and her local community youth worker. Leigh's home/school support worker has contacts with all these and has visited Leigh at home regularly. Leigh's mother feels that she has never fully come to terms with her experiences and should receive counselling, but Leigh refuses all offers of help.

Her home/school support worker arranged for her to have some work sent home and, because Leigh will not attend school, she has arranged for her to see a youth counsellor through her local community health service. It took several home visits and chats with Leigh to persuade her to attend and, during these visits, Leigh revealed that she has also been bullied on the school bus. Her fears about attending school stem from this and her reluctance to tell her mother from her desire not to heap further worries on her.

Leigh's home/school support worker has supported Sara in imposing strict boundaries on Leigh and whom she sees, and Leigh is now seeing her counsellor regularly. Leigh was also clearly given support with being able to feel safe on the school bus without the risk of bullying. The school ensured that this was appropriately dealt with.

Points for practice

In this case study, the home/school worker liaised with other statutory workers and the parent to try to resolve the most obvious difficulties Leigh was experiencing. By working with Sara, Leigh's mother, the home/school worker encouraged strategies that effectively made Leigh feel safe and looked after by her mother. This then enabled Leigh to feel confident enough to say why she really didn't want to attend school. Also, Leigh's long-term issues were supported alongside the short-term needs, enabling progress to be made in all areas of Leigh's life. This included counselling to help her understand her experiences and should also include support to address her alcohol misuse.

This was clearly a long-term process which enabled Leigh to re-establish links with her school. In this situation, the home/school worker facilitated this through:

- working with other statutory agencies
- supporting Sara, the mother
- additional access to resources, i.e. counselling
- collaborating with the school.

You can see that this case study appeared quite straightforward initially, but actually required multi-layered intervention before all the issues could be resolved.

Being healthy

Home/school support can be part of the healthy schools agenda, by providing outreach opportunities into the community to encourage healthy lifestyle choices. While identification of individual families who have health concerns may provide targeted offers of assistance, other work that is generally encouraging of healthy choices can impact on many families and encourage those already working to improve their health.

Close links with school nurses, health visitors, local GP surgeries and health promotion projects are valuable in bringing a healthy agenda into school. Home/school support workers should be viewed as part of a team within schools and workloads should be tailored accordingly.

Identification

Families that may require targeted work to encourage healthy lifestyle changes include:

- families with obesity issues
- families with poor nutrition because of transport or financial difficulties
- families with chronic health conditions, both physical and mental; affecting adults or children
- whole community health issues, such as poor diet, smoking and alcohol misuse, lack of exercise, mental health issues.

Interventions

Once identified, home/school support work can include any of the following interventions:

- Involvement of outside health agencies through direct referrals or planned events for parents, e.g. dental hygienist visiting school to speak with parents and children.
- Working with individual families to access advice and encourage take up of health appointments.

- Working with groups of parents on targeted issues, e.g. healthy eating for toddlers, good packed lunches, exercise and children.
- One-off events, e.g. fruit tasting, walking or exercising events.
- Introducing health agendas to different groups, e.g. mother and toddler, breakfast clubs, school councils.

Enjoy and achieve

In the majority of cases, it is probably safe to say that very unhappy children do not achieve as well as they could if they were emotionally stable and content. Children who are anxious or upset are unlikely to be able to concentrate and learn. Referrals to home/school support workers from teachers may often simply be: 'he doesn't seem happy at all and can't concentrate on his work'. There may be many reasons for a child to be unhappy and unable to concentrate. Anxiety and unhappiness may be:

- **transient**, following a crisis or event, e.g. bereavement or loss
- **social**, concerning a child's difficulties with friendships, bullying, etc.
- **educational**, concerning a child's difficulties with learning due to a specific real or perceived problem, e.g. undisclosed hearing difficulty
- **chronic**, due to an unresolved family or out-of-school problem
- **age dependent**, as maturity brings anxieties that younger children were not aware of, and younger children may worry about things they don't understand.

Identification

Again, referrals from teaching and support staff form the basis for identification (see Appendix 1), but other indicators should be considered:

- parental concerns; listening to parents
- children who show a marked change in mood
- children who show slow or no academic progress for no clear reason.

Interventions

Close working with parents should always be the rule where a child is failing to achieve. This could include the wider family network, such as grandparents, aunts and uncles who may be able to offer sensitive support. Child protection issues should be considered, and encouraging the child to talk through problems in school with a suitable, well-trained and trusted staff member will give the child opportunity for disclosure should he wish.

More general interventions could include:

1 Any intervention that raises educational standards and expectations within a family, e.g. further education and career development, including basic literacy and numeracy, computing, links to colleges and career advice.
2 Home visits and opportunities for children and families to voice concerns and problems.
3 Help with crises and self-referrals to other agencies.
4 Celebration of successes however small.

Making a positive contribution

With enjoyment and achievement comes the possibility of real contribution to the community, including the right to voice opinions and be listened to. Isolation within a community may lead to individuals suffering without cause because no one is aware of their difficulties. This can be particularly true of migrant and refugee communities where the benefits and rights available to them are unknown. Once a family is encouraged to join in with their community, then opportunities arise to promote greater well-being, not just for those specific individuals, but for the whole community. Their contribution may prove invaluable to many others. Some home/school support workers are members of minority communities who have themselves experienced isolation and deprivation, and are now using their skills to benefit others. Encouraging full membership of a community through the school may involve any number of innovative ideas. Examples of successful interventions are:

- parent forums and councils
- student councils
- mentoring schemes
- community arts groups and theatre productions
- community newspapers and websites mindful of minority languages
- parent involvement in schools through help in classrooms, extracurricular activities, etc.
- trips and outings for families
- extended family involvement, e.g. grandparents
- volunteering within the community and the school, including friendship schemes and local volunteer agencies. Further information about volunteering can be found at the following website: www.volunteering.org.uk

The potential in this area is limited only by the imagination of the school team and the parents and families themselves.

Achieve economic well-being

With many home/school support schemes centred on areas where deprivation, underachievement, poverty and dependence on benefits are common problems, this may be one of the hardest targets to attempt to improve. Unemployment and poor expectation may be generational with families never having experienced financial stability or full employment. Other barriers include language and literacy difficulties, housing problems and poor access to services and transport. One parent found that to get to an interview to ascertain what benefits were due involved a 45-minute bus ride costing £5.50 which at the time he didn't have.

Home/school support can offer a twofold approach to these problems: firstly, helping families to raise the expectations of their children and, secondly, to offer practical help in tackling the educational and economic difficulties of the parents. Interventions could include:

- Support and referrals to other agencies to help access appropriate help, e.g. debt counselling, benefits access, housing. This could involve attending meetings with parents or funding transport costs.
- Adult education information and support to start on a course.

- Self-esteem work of any kind with both parents and children.
- Support for transition to secondary school and further education where costs may be high and there are risks of disaffection.

Points for practice
1 Understanding families
The structure of the family and its members cultural background will undoubtedly influence the way in which a home/school worker can approach and engage with them. Working with traveller families, for example, is significantly different from working with local settled communities. Traveller communities are also diverse, and working with Roma travellers will require different knowledge and skills to working with Irish travellers. Individual communities may require a dedicated liaison worker to help break down barriers of cultural misunderstanding and isolation, and many of these workers come from the communities themselves, giving them intimate knowledge of the most significant problems.

Extended families are often crucial to solving problems. For some families, finding the significant adult who will initiate a solution to a problem may be a necessary exercise in patience and persistence. Even in the most extreme of dysfunctional families, there may be one person to whom children can turn for support and practical help, and finding that person can increase a child's chance of sustaining educational involvement. So home/school support sometimes consists of working closely with grandparents, aunts and uncles and even older siblings. In one instance, for example, it was an older sister who learned how to groom a child for head lice and keep them free from further infection.

2 Continuity
Home/school working encompasses the most trivial and the most difficult issues. Remember, even when there are other agencies involved and serious interventions taking place, the children still come into school. Most schools will have a complement of 'Looked After Children' (LAC) and children at various stages of Social Services' interventions. Home/school workers are increasingly used as the link person with agencies and are included in multi-agency working for families in crisis.

Each set of family circumstances impacts and affects a child and where problems arise and parents struggle to cope, or tragedy strikes and family life is fragile, the child may still be brought to school and required to cope. At such crisis points, a familiar person in school who regularly helps in small ways and is always willing to listen may be the first port of call, either to offer practical solutions or simply to listen.

When outside agencies and interventions are over, school remains a constant. A home/school support worker represents a long-term contact, getting to know families over considerable periods of time and celebrating successes as well as supporting through crises.

3 Referrals
Referrals fall into three main categories: parent self-referrals, child self-referrals and staff referrals.

Parent self-referrals will be more common as parents become aware that help is available in school and come to know the individual home/school worker. Word of mouth will often disseminate this information, but newsletters and specific information leaflets about the role of a home/school worker are important. Parent information should make clear that the worker is able to help with issues above and beyond schooling and has access to interagency support. It should bear in mind the possibility of language barriers and use translations or pictures.

Some staff referrals are initially parent self-referrals passed on to the home/school worker where appropriate. If a parent mentions to a teacher that they are suffering domestic violence, for example, the teacher may then suggest a visit to the worker for confidential help.

Child self-referrals may involve issues around school or out of school, such as bullying, friendship issues, crises at home. Again, this may initially be disclosed through a teacher and the home/school worker may then have a role in contacting parents and offering appropriate help and support. Once established, home/school workers are often approached by children with problems as they are seen as a neutral member of staff. There are obvious child protection implications in the role and it is important that home/school workers are trained and supported appropriately.

Child self-referrals are particularly high in secondary schools where home/school workers, mentors and pastoral support staff work more directly with children.

Staff referrals may centre on concerns expressed by children or their parents or may come from knowledge picked up from other parents or staff members. A staff member may have concerns about sudden changes in behaviour, general well-being, presentation in school, tiredness, inability to concentrate or changes in health. Once a referral has been made, the parent/carer is contacted. The worker must raise the concerns in a way that is sensitive and non-judgemental. Handling these referrals requires good teamworking, where staff must judge situations and communicate information confidentially and appropriately (see Appendix 1). Information from several staff members may highlight concerns. Such a case may be when a lunchtime supervisor notices a child refusing food, and then a teacher notes the same child is lethargic and finds it hard to concentrate. A sensitive phone call home by the home/school support worker may allow a parent to discuss concerns about eating and how they and their child can access help.

In any school, regular discussion with staff should take place to encourage good practice and share information. A referrer should expect feedback, even if it is only to say that the parent has requested confidentiality but the problem is being addressed.

Signposting and multi-agency working

Signposting refers to the practice of directing families to agencies where relevant help or support may be accessed. When this is effective, school becomes a centre where parents can find help for issues as diverse as housing, mental health, local libraries and adult learning opportunities. Local agencies are usually willing to supply information leaflets, contact details and to visit schools, giving parents an opportunity to ask questions and seek help. Home/school workers keep and update contact details from many agencies and with experience will get to know who the most appropriate contacts are.

Multi-agency working is an increasing part of all children's services with central and local government initiatives seeking to link service providers to better facilitate delivery. Multi-agency working divides into two main areas:

1   Those interventions described above where initiative comes from the home/ school worker and is strengthened by networking meetings, and area meetings with other similar workers to exchange information.
2   Multi-agency working forms part of the school agenda where external agencies have input into home/school worker's referrals. These might include Social Services, health visitors, SureStart, Connexions and community policing.

Working with other agencies has sometimes proved difficult, because of failure by these agencies to recognize and understand the role played by the home/ school worker. Hopefully, wider knowledge of the role and appreciation of its function is overcoming ignorance in this area.

Extended schools

Extended schools here refers to the practice of using a school as a resource within the community, offering the skills and facilities to enhance the quality of a community. The Extended Schools prospectus (DfES, June 2005) sets out a range of services that should be accessible through all schools by 2010. Home/school support workers working directly with families are an integral part of extended schools. Working with groups of parents, they provide three main parent services:

1   **Social and recreational**, from tea and chat drop-ins to aromatherapy.
2   **Self-improvement and parenting**, including health and well-being, family nutrition and cookery and parenting courses, targeting different age groups and transitions.
3   **Further education and career development**, including basic literacy and numeracy, computing, links to colleges and career advice.

Social and recreational groups provide a forum for ideas and mutual support. They nurture valuable friendships and encourage self-esteem and community links. Many such groups move on naturally to include self-improvement courses, discussions on health and social issues, and invite health visitors, dental nurses, nutritionists and other professionals to speak at meetings.

It is often noted that involvement in groups such as these progresses from the social, through self-improvement, to the educational and career prospects where quality of life is enhanced.

Meeting local needs

Many home/school support workers initiate events and activities that are directly relevant to their local community needs. These may include dieting and healthy living groups, social events and family trips, gardening and conservation projects, multicultural and language events, and community arts. Uniquely placed within the community, home/school support can be reactive to community needs and proactive in anticipating concerns.

Health, safety and well-being

The role of a home/school worker has been explored in some detail, giving a broad picture of the duties and aims, as well as the type of problem-solving skills the job entails. While other jobs do deal directly with families and children and include home visiting, escorting to meetings, etc., home/school support is a very broad remit and takes place in establishments where education is the main aim, and not social welfare. Issues of health and personal safety are similar to those experienced by workers in other caring professions, but as the role is new and has evolved often independently from within a school or district, then the provision of training, support and supervision has often been patchy or inadequate.

In this section, therefore, the main issues around health, personal safety and well-being are examined, highlighting the need for better support for individuals carrying out these roles.

Issues of health and well-being fall into three main areas. These can be summarized as:

1   workload pressure
2   isolation within post
3   safety aspects of lone working.

To take each individually:

1   *Workload pressure* can occur whenever the role is needs-led. Where the need is great, it is inevitable that pressure will build to meet that need, particularly as it involves the well-being of children. Schools have often appointed a home/school worker precisely because there is a high level of social need within the local community. The appointment seeks to address this need with the resources available to the school in terms of personnel, hours and finance. In areas of social deprivation, resources are rarely proportional to need. People appointed to these roles have a genuine desire to help others and are competent at coping with situations requiring high levels of concentration, listening and patience. In responding to such situations, it is easy to become over-committed and stretched beyond time-allotted and personal resources.

Points for practice
Good training in personal timetabling, support and supervision where workloads are heavy and a strong pastoral support team within the school all help to alleviate this.

2   *Isolation* can follow on from this high-level pressure of work. Schools concerned with meeting educational targets, attendance rates and special provision may appoint a single individual to a home/school link post and

require that person to work independently for the majority of their hours. If adequate provision is not made to network within school, to link up with teaching and non-teaching staff and to form strong bonds with colleagues, then the worker will feel lonely, isolated and unsupported. Furthermore, without these opportunities staff members may fail to understand the nature of the role, fail to appreciate the work that is being done and consequently fail to refer appropriately.

Points for practice
To prevent isolation from occurring, the following are recommended:

1 Each home/school worker should have at least two staff members with whom she can meet regularly and who will respond immediately should she need support in an emergency.
2 A regular meeting should take place with management to review the extent and detail of the work being done.
3 Home/school workers should be actively integrated into schools and be enabled to link with other members of staff both professionally and socially.
4 An individual should be appointed to make sure that the home/school worker is kept aware of dates, decisions, etc. made in school.

3 *Safety* aspects are the same as for other professionals working with vulnerable families. They include:

(a) *Having an awareness of danger.* Awareness of possible dangers allows those dangers to be minimized or eliminated, and regular support from the management team in school will reinforce this and maintain vigilance. The preventable dangers are most obviously to do with violent or abusive clients, but these are not the only considerations. Workers may be exposing themselves to environments that are dangerous or unpleasant in other ways. Everything from the risk of accidental injury from needles to dangerous dogs and passive smoking has been mentioned, and it is worth stating here that some schools will not ask workers to visit because of the difficulties posed by such risks (see Appendix 2).

Points for practice
In these situations, adequate provision for private client interviews at school is made, or the worker may meet clients in a neutral location such as a café.

(b) *Carrying out responsible risk assessments* when visiting or meeting clients, notification of whereabouts and ensuring ease of contact.

Points for practice
Risk assessments can include a strategic phone call from the key staff member in school to ensure that the visit is progressing well; it should also include a set time to finish, preventing a visit from running over into free time or other

tasks. Training in risk assessment and personal safety should be obligatory for all workers undertaking visiting and meeting clients alone or out of school.

(c) Home/school workers should be issued with a *mobile phone* and should notify a key staff member of their movements, particularly when visiting homes.

(d) Home/school workers should always be aware that there is an *emotional strain* attached to some referrals, where a family becomes increasingly vulnerable and situations deteriorate.

Points for practice
Workers should be adequately supervised while dealing with these cases, and support should come from a strong well-trained child protection team within the school management system. Home/school workers frequently tread a fine line between personal welfare and client need, especially where there are serious concerns about the vulnerability of children. It is important not to compromise personal health and well-being in these situations, as a worker who is unable to cope or overstretched is ill-equipped to make judgements. A strong and well-trained pastoral support team that is kept well informed of developments will provide balance and consideration where difficult problems arise.

(e) It is important to remember that there may already be appropriate management channels for referrals in schools for Social Services, mental health services and police, for example. These members of staff should be well informed of any developments and will be able to make value judgements.

Points for practice
It is not advisable that home/school support workers should also hold the position of Child Protection Officer and have responsibility for child protection referrals as this may seriously compromise their relationships with all parents. Having said this, child protection concerns should always be central to the role and home/school support workers share a responsibility with all school staff to ensure the safety of children.

The qualities of a home/school support worker need to be many. A home/support worker needs to:

- believe totally in their work
- enjoy working with children
- enjoy working with families
- enjoy and have the confidence to work with para-professionals.

They need to be:

- good listeners
- able to keep confidences
- proactive
- able to ask for assistance

- aware of dangers to themselves, as well as to children and families
- good organizers
- good time-keepers
- able to work independently and as part of a team.

Indeed, it is a role which requires many personal qualities and needs to be given professional standing.

 Summary

It is hoped that this chapter has highlighted the complexity and intensity of the role and responsibilities of home/school support workers. If schools and local communities decide to invest in such a position, it is vital that they are willing to be fully involved in the development and maintenance of the role. Schools, and senior managers and governors in particular, need to recognize that the whole school community will need to understand, support and be able to recognize the importance of such a role. The need for training, supervision and resources must be fully recognized prior to the appointment of a home/school worker, if the position is going to be effective and professionally managed.

∿ Points for reflection

1 Reflect on the qualities you consider you have to enable you to be an efficient and effective home/school support worker.
2 Who in a mainstream primary school could take on this time-consuming and vital role? Is there a staff member in place already, or would a new appointment be necessary?
3 Consider carefully whether the school you are working in, or have applied to work for, has the systems in place necessary to support a home/school worker when complex and difficult cases arise. Write a list of essentials, such as a mobile phone and a private room, and a list of desirable equipment, resources or systems.
4 Do you think that a home/school support worker should be given professional standing? State your reasons clearly whether supporting or arguing against the question posed.

 Further reading

Department for Education and Skills (2003) *Every Child Matters*. London: TSO.

Department of Health (2002) *Working with Children in Need and their Families: Draft consultation document*. London: The Department of Health. www.dh.gov.uk/en/ Publicationsandstatistics/Publications/PublicationsPolicyAndGuidance/DH_4005215

HM Government (2006) *What to do if You're Worried a Child is Being Abused: Every Child Matters, Change for Children.* Annesley: DfES. www.everychildmatters.gov.uk/_files/34C 39F24E7EF47FBA9139FA01C7B0370.pdf

HMSO (2006) *Working Together to Safeguard Children: A guide to inter-agency working to safeguard and promote the welfare of children.* London: TSO.

 Useful websites

Parent Associations

Direct Gov – www.direct.gov.uk/en/EducationAndLearning/Schools/SchoolLife/DG_ 4016015

National Confederation of Parent Teacher Associations – www.ncpta.org.uk

Traveller Family Information

Becta Inclusion Website – http://inclusion.ngfl.gov.uk

Becta Traveller Education Pages – http://lists.becta.org.uk/mailman/listinfo/trav-ed

National Association of Teachers of Travellers – www.natt.org.uk/2006/index.php?pk=8

Romani online magazine – www.geocities.com/daveauss/indexpics/Romaniworld.pdf

2

Domestic Violence

> **This chapter will discuss the issues surrounding domestic violence. It will provide advice about how school/parent support workers can access services such as Social Services, police and housing agencies, and will explore family anxiety and self-esteem issues and their impact on children's learning.**

The amended Children Act 1989 recognizes the harm caused to children living with domestic violence. In defining the harm, it includes 'impairment suffered from seeing or hearing the ill treatment of another' (Adoption and Children Act, 2002).

Statistics for children impacted by domestic violence are extrapolated from surveys and research on domestic violence and women. The 2001 British Crime Survey (BCS) indicated that more than one in five women (21%) and one in ten men (1%) have experienced at least one incident of domestic violence since the age of 16. The 1996 British Crime Survey found that half of those suffering domestic violence had children living with them who were under the age of 16 (Mullender, 2004).

Mullender et al. (2002) also found that children are nearly always aware of the violence, however hard parents might try to conceal it from them. If they are not physically present when the violence takes place, then they are usually aware of the atmosphere, tension and injuries that result from it. Home/school support must be holistic when attempting to provide guidance to families suffering in this way. It is important for home/school support workers to understand that domestic violence presents a unique set of problems for schools and requires great care to ensure the safety of the worker and the family concerned.

Domestic violence can manifest in many forms. The Home Office defines domestic violence as:

> any violence between current and former partners in an intimate relationship, wherever the violence occurs. The violence may include physical, sexual, emotional and financial abuse. (Downloaded on 19.08.2007: www.crimereduction.gov.uk/dv/dv03a.htm#4)

Every Child Matters

Children are profoundly affected by their home environment and the effects of domestic violence will undoubtedly impact on their ability to concentrate and hence learn in school. Feelings of guilt, anxiety and frustration dominate, and where the violence has been prolonged, children find normal relationships with peers and staff difficult. Some children also present as being tightly controlled, as keeping secrets and as maintaining appearances in public. Focusing on the Every Child Matters agenda, domestic violence can and will seriously disrupt a child's long-term educational and social outcomes. School may represent a safe and constant haven where interventions to support the family and alleviate the effects of the violence have some chance of success.

Being healthy

Domestic violence impacts on health in several ways. Where families are still experiencing violence, perpetrator control may affect their ability to access health services. Children suffering the stress of domestic violence may be sleep-deprived, constantly anxious and poorly nourished. Anxiety will affect children's appetite, any stress-related illnesses such as eczema and asthma, and their concentration and vigilance, making them more prone to accidents. Where children are themselves physically abused, they may present with untreated injuries and bruising.

Identification

Identifying child victims of domestic violence depends primarily on disclosure, but strong indicators exist in health and physical presentation as well as in their behaviour and emotional well-being. The following symptoms indicate problems in general, and working with parents should *not* be compromised because of suspicions that may prove ill-founded. Children suffering anxiety for any number of reasons may present with the following:

- panic attacks or unexplained crying
- physical symptoms of anxiety and stress, eczema, bedwetting, wetting in school, asthma, tiredness, sleep disturbance and sleep deprivation
- poor concentration and lack of academic progress.

Interventions

Any sign of physical distress should be followed up. Where children are suffering harm from domestic violence, a victim will often disclose this when her children are seen to be suffering. If this does not happen, no harm is done by highlighting a child's poor health in school and offering the support of the school nurse or Child and Adolescent Mental Health Services (CAMHS). A parent can at worse deny there is a problem and at best acknowledge what is going on and accept help. Important information should be noted and filed where there are suspicions of any kind of domestic problem. A proforma has been included for recording small incidents and keeping track of concerns (see Appendix 3).

Interventions should be clear and robust, and could include the following:

- clear offers of help discreetly and confidentially presented
- referrals to other agencies where this is seen as relevant
- clear and confidential recording of concerns around both physical and mental health
- a school culture of not ignoring concerns, but of referring on and reporting where worries arise.

Being safe

The threat to both the physical and emotional safety of children living with domestic violence can be summarized as follows:

1 *Witnessed violence* either physical or emotional
2 *Violence towards the child* either physical or emotional
3 *Violence committed by a child* either physical or emotional
4 *Transient incidents* of any kind where the violence is outside the normal family experience.

These categories are not exclusive and may overlap considerably.

Witnessed violence involves a child seeing one family member humiliate or hurt another often from a position of powerlessness. Where the situation has been continuous throughout the child's life, he may never have experienced a peaceful family situation. They may be co-opted into that violence or assume a similar role to the perpetrator as they grow older. They may attempt to defend the victim and comfort and protect younger siblings. Even where the parents insist they never fight in front of the children, the children will often know and be affected by the atmosphere and aftermath. There will be long-term effects on the child throughout his life and his ability to cope in school may be seriously affected.

Violence towards the child may occur as a result of a child attempting to intervene to protect a parent or as part of the bigger picture of violence in the household. Disclosure of violence towards a child may come from the child himself, from a family member or friend, or as a result of a chance discovery. School child protection procedures must then be followed and schools are required to notify relevant authorities (i.e. police and Social Services). However, in real situations disclosures that are clear-cut are rare and regular staff training is crucial in effective handling of these events.

Depending on the age of the child, *violence committed by a child* may be classified as behaviour problems, assault or abuse. Where a child has serious behaviour problems, they may be lashing out at home hurting parents or siblings, or they may be terrorizing the family with threats of violence and extreme behaviour. Parents in this situation often come to school for help, and referrals to relevant agencies can then be made. This will be considered in greater depth in Chapter 6, but mention here is vital because of the impact it has on the family, and because it may reflect more general or historic domestic violence.

Transient incidents are important to pay attention to, especially as they are so frequently reported in school. They range from violence brought about by a stressful situation in a household to neighbour disputes and family fights at parties. One child reported violence every time there was a family celebration; his family did not seem to be able to meet up without revisiting old quarrels and having a seriously big fight. This would sometimes result in hospitalization or imprisonment or both and was very traumatic for the child. In normal circumstances, the home was peaceful and the child came to dread family get-togethers.

Interventions

These must centre around the safety of the child and rely on the child being able to acknowledge the violence. Within the safety of the school, it may be possible for the child to discuss the violence at home and then appropriate suggestions can be made about safety. Most interventions will involve clear referrals where child safety is at risk. The following suggestions should be considered:

- Schools must have clear referral procedures that involve the notification of the partner/spouse who is the victim. Where a child is deemed to be at risk, consideration must be made as to the means of communicating with the victim. Ringing the home may not be an option, for example.
- Schools may have to draw up clear plans to prevent perpetrators from finding or accessing victims and children.
- Families can be encouraged to have emergency plans that involve notifying police and Social Services, and finding somewhere safe to go should the perpetrator find them or become violent towards them.
- Home/school support *must* be clear and bounded and should not take the place of statutory authorities, such as police or Social Services.

 Case study: Craig, aged 8

Craig's father is an alcoholic and when drunk subjects Craig's mother to verbal and physical attacks. She has put up with this and his control of her life for 14 years. In school, Craig has been withdrawn and upset, often sobbing for no reason. His older brother Lee is physically violent with other children and gets angry without provocation. At no point would either of the boys admit to any problems at home and their mother was called to school on several occasions and stated that she didn't know why the boys were behaving in this way. She finally admitted the problem when Craig tried to protect her from his father and was injured by him.

Points for practice

This case study illustrates clearly how much will be hidden until an injury to a child actually occurs. The situation once admitted will need extremely careful and well-planned support for all the family, at a pace that the mother can make successfully. It is clear that when the time is appropriate, the mother and the boys will most probably need to leave the family home for a place of safety. This will require financial and housing support. The boys will need long-term counselling and support with their education to try to ensure they can recover from the family experiences. This counselling may take place in school or it may be provided by an outside agency such as CAMHS. At no stage, however, must the home/school support worker try to encourage particular actions without statutory agency support and careful consideration and planning, or go and talk to the father. Referrals to other agencies are likely to be required.

 Case study: Peter, aged 11

Peter's father is controlling and obsessive. He dominates the family and insists on very strict standards of behaviour and tidiness. When he is challenged, he has violent rages or becomes withdrawn and ill. Peter's mother and siblings all comply with his wishes in order to keep the peace. Peter's father puts enormous pressure on Peter to succeed and Peter is anxious and nervous about examinations. He doesn't have friends round to visit and doesn't seem to enjoy any subject at school, although he does well in most.

Points for practice

In such a situation, where Peter is clearly suffering emotional and perhaps also physical violence, the home/school support worker needs to try to encourage him to attend clubs after school, so that he can have opportunities to broaden his social skills and network, and also learn to enjoy an activity in a safe and secure environment. This may also be a situation where trying to encourage and engage Peter's mother in school life would help her to begin to address her family's needs. Of course if any evidence of physical violence becomes apparent then child protection procedures must be initiated immediately.

Enjoy and achieve

There are many factors in life that might adversely affect a child's ability to engage and learn in school. These include:

- family breakdown
- parents working long hours
- poverty and low expectation.

However, domestic violence is particularly destructive and disruptive to a child's education.

Identification

1   Where domestic violence is ongoing and undetected, the child may present with a variety of difficulties, from anxiety and tiredness, to extreme anger

and violence, and school services are at a loss to understand why. Domestic violence is by nature secret and breaking this silence is very difficult.

2   Where domestic violence is ongoing and acknowledged, the child may be able to speak to peers or staff members. The child may also be ashamed, victimized in school, and isolated, feeling themselves set apart by their circumstances.

3   Where domestic violence is present, but the victim is taking steps to resolve the issue and move on, then the presentation of the child may be one of conflicting loyalties, dread of crises should plans be found out and confusion if they have not been told of the changing situation. If the school is unaware of the situation, then the child's behaviour can be misinterpreted or challenged leading to further anxiety.

4   Where the family have moved on from the violence, there may still be considerable dangers. Many women suffer continued violence and threats from partners long after they have separated. If contact has been agreed, then the children may still be living with confusion and conflicting loyalties. If children have been in refuges or moving to avoid danger from a violent partner, then schooling may have been seriously disrupted with educational and social consequences.

While Social Services, police and voluntary/charitable groups may have been involved with a family during crises and withdraw once things are seen as more stable, school is a constant and represents a unique opportunity to offer more long-term support and help.

Each child within a family affected by violence reacts in line with his or her character, social abilities and understanding, age and position in the family and identification with either parent. Certain patterns of behaviour are repeated in children in school and some are listed below:

- general anxiety about what is happening at home, including separation anxiety and especially age-inappropriate clinging to a parent and, in extremes, school refusing
- causal inferences ('something I have done has caused this') and assumption of responsibility
- guilt and shame
- secrecy and isolation ('friends can't come round and I don't talk about home')
- poor academic progress out of step with apparent intelligence
- friendship problems
- over protectiveness and anxiety about siblings
- controlled or obsessive behaviour around appearance, belongings, keeping appointments, etc.

This is by no means a list of indicators. It is also important to bear in mind that many of these behaviours are indicative of anxiety in childhood for reasons other than domestic violence.

Some children will show little apparent effect from experiencing violence at home. These children may have coping strategies and/or personality traits that enable them to withstand the worst effects, along with people they can turn to for support. They may be able to treat school as a safe haven where normality and predictability provide comfort. Dedicated home/school support workers may offer a unique opportunity to these children to maintain some stability and talk openly about their problems.

 Case study: Jack, aged 15

Jack's mother had fled a violent relationship when her partner threatened to burn the house down and poured petrol on the living room floor. Jack was in the middle of his GCSE mocks at the time, and he and his mother and three younger siblings found themselves staying in a bed and break-fast several miles from his school. His mother was able to drive him into school, but he had no clean clothes with him and no school uniform.

Points for practice

Listening to the situation carefully is the first priority. Then ensuring Jack's examinations are not affected is the next important matter to solve. A home/school support worker in this situation should arrange for a set of uniform clothes to be kept at school for Jack, and also provide him with pencils, calcu-lator, etc. for the examinations. This organized, the worker can try to access funds for Jack's lunches and also help his mother to find charity funds to buy the children clothes while she waits for benefits to be paid. Jack was able to tell a few select friends about his circumstances, but the home/school support worker ensured he was available to talk to when Jack needed him. In this way, the immediate issues were quickly dealt with, ensuring Jack could continue without embarrassment at school. Longer-term support might be required to cope with the emotional trauma.

Interventions

Interventions to help children will depend upon the current circumstances of the family. The following are a few possible options available.

1   Where the violence is ongoing and unacknowledged and school has only mis-givings and suspicions about the possibility of violence, then support is lim-ited to offering opportunities to confide, giving space to think and be calm and intervening to address the symptoms. Acknowledge that you have noticed that a child is always tired, worried, cries for nothing or needs to con-tact a parent during the day. Make sure that the child knows you are available to speak to in confidence and that you can offer help in all kinds of situations. Work together with class teachers, teaching assistants, lunchtime supervisors, etc. to keep a record of the problems that arise and that might add to a bigger picture of concern. If children do disclose domestic violence, it is vital that they are believed and taken seriously.

2   Where violence is ongoing and known to be so then a more open approach may be taken. Notifying those members of staff that need to know and mak-ing sure they understand the confidential nature of this information can

prevent a child being told off for something they can't help. Children may come in with homework unfinished and equipment missing, and discreetly helping to solve this keeps a child engaged with school.

3 Where violence is ongoing, but the victim is taking steps to escape, then children often present as deeply disturbed and worried. Parents may arrive at school suddenly during the day to take a child while a partner is at work. Children may have moved schools several times and be unsure of friendships, academic work, uniform and equipment. They may be living in inadequate accommodation with little access to washing facilities and no privacy for homework or personal life. They may be aware of the necessity to keep quiet about their circumstances and worry about being found out. There may be issues around access, continued conflict around custody and financial worries; all these things will unsettle and worry children.

4 Those children who are in families that have broken away from violent relationships and are living more stable lives still need support and help to deal with feelings and emotions. These children may benefit from a range of opportunities of counselling and therapy in school. The 'surviving' parent may also need help with parenting, counselling and financial advice, all of which could be accessed through school with the help of the home/school support worker.

Support for children in school can take the form of counselling, play therapy, small group work, life-story work and safety and crisis planning. It aims to help the child in the following ways:

- to rebuild self-esteem
- to reassure a child that what has happened was not his fault
- to give him permission to talk about his experiences in a safe and confidential environment
- to learn that he is not alone and that others are experiencing similar problems
- to help him formulate realistic safety plans.

Home/school workers may be qualified to take on some of this work or may facilitate outside agencies and specialist services to work with the children. Linking regularly with the parent and reassuring them that school is taking the problem seriously, believes them and supports their children gives vital confidence to parents and children. Working with children in these circumstances is skilled work and should not be undertaken without appropriate training and supervision.

Making a positive contribution

For families trying to manage and cope with domestic violence, this may involve the simple expedient of being welcomed and treated as normal within the school community. Domestic violence may be controlling and stifling of talent and initiative, and offering a person an opportunity to join in and play a role in school is a positive and empowering step.

Victims are frequently prevented from approaching others, working or having their own money, accessing further education or health services. Once they have moved on from the violence, the confidence of the whole family may be shattered and any work that aims to rebuild this may be beneficial.

Some suggested interventions may be:

- invitations to the parent to help in school
- small groups that promote self-esteem for parent victims and children
- safe and accessible adult education courses
- good listening so that the home/school support worker responds to the real needs of the family.

Achieving economic well-being

The disruption and isolation of domestic violence frequently leads escaping families into financial insecurity. Reasons include poor uptake of benefits due to moving around and problems finding employment. Children may suffer disruption in their education, jeopardizing their chances of examination success and further education.

Home/school support can put in place practical measures to enable families to keep in touch with education and enhance their educational prospects. Support may include:

1 Providing transport and equipment for a child at crucial times, such as examinations, transition, sporting activities and interviews.
2 Providing transport for the parent to get to important appointments; helping with completion of forms and telephone calls.
3 Providing in-school access to adult education.
4 Through extended schools and good safety plans providing adequate childcare and after-school activities.

Home/school support can offer advice for those parents planning to leave a violent partner on how to begin to secure some financial independence. This advice is available through independent charities, websites, the Citizens Advice Bureau and Social Services. The threat of poverty, shared debt and inability to provide for children are major reasons for staying in abusive relationships, and many people attempt to leave only to find that their financial position on their own is untenable. Simple measures like setting up a separate bank account and getting a part-time job can begin the process. Legal help is needed to divide assets and savings and to decide entitlements. Where utility bills and debts are concerned, it is important to notify companies and banks that you are no longer living at an address and are not responsible for payments. Once separated from a partner, a person may be entitled to income support and tax credits, and contacting the Benefits Agency and Inland Revenue to arrange payments should be a priority.

Multi-agency working

Successful interventions to address domestic violence require the help of more than one agency. The following information may help home/school support workers to understand the position of victims and liaise with relevant authorities.

Housing
Local authority
Where it is necessary for a parent and children to leave their home, they are entitled to temporary accommodation through the local authority, Homeless Person's Unit. This accommodation may be very basic, is often inadequate for any length of time and families are reluctant to swap a known risk for an unknown bed and breakfast far from their children's school and any support from relatives. By law, local authorities must avoid placing families in bed and breakfast accommodation (Homelessness Act 2002) but in reality this is still a problem.

Housing departments
These can be very helpful in the long term where finding a separate home is necessary, and home/school support workers may be involved in accompanying a parent to a meeting, helping them to plan a move or finding voluntary agencies that can help locally.

Family support
Family support is often the most successful means of escaping domestic violence; taking temporary refuge with a family member or friend allows plans to be made and better accommodation to be found. It also provides a degree of protection against the perpetrator.

Refuges
These can be accessed through the national domestic violence free phone helpline, 0808 2000 247, run by the Women's Aid and Refuge charities. They will offer places in refuges to women and children, although some will not take boys over 12 years. Places may be scarce in an area and it may be necessary for the family to travel long distances. Again, this can be a barrier to taking up this kind of help. Refuges are at secret locations and have access to help for women wanting to rebuild their lives. They can usually offer financial and housing advice, and health and counselling information.

It may be desirable for a victim to evict a violent partner from the property and legal advice on how to do this is available through local Police Domestic Violence Units. How difficult and practical it is will depend on the nature of the ownership or tenancy, as well as the risk the perpetrator might pose.

Permanently re-housing a family will depend very much on their circumstances and specialist help can be sought through the National Domestic Violence Helpline, Shelter or the local Citizen's Advice Bureau. The local authority housing department is also very helpful.

Legal
Accessing the legal system will be either through the police (criminal law) or a solicitor (civil law).

1   The police can press charges against a perpetrator and it is their decision based on evidence available. Domestic Violence or Community Safety Units

within the police can offer victims help to keep safe. They may offer advice on changing locks and they may caution the offender if he approaches the victim. If the perpetrator has been charged and bailed, the police may be able to order him to stay away from the victim.

2   Under civil law, a solicitor can help a victim to apply for an injunction to restrict the perpetrator and prevent him from approaching the victim. Legal restrictions on access to children may also be put in place and school should be notified if this is the case. A parent may apply for a residence order or a supervised contact order to prevent a partner from accessing the children. It may be necessary to prevent a parent from picking children up from school and there should be a legal basis for this either through civil or criminal law. School can then respond to any attempts to access the children with a call to the police.

Solicitors specialize in different fields and a local area should have lists of solicitors specializing in domestic violence, divorce and separation available through the police, housing or local charities. Help with costs will depend on income and assets, and again a solicitor will be able to access legal aid if a victim is entitled to this.

Other help

Using Social Services for help often proves difficult with families reluctant to involve them for fear of family and friends finding out and the stigma attached to this, and in extreme cases fear of children being removed. Home/school support workers are uniquely placed to begin to change some of these attitudes and encourage families to see Social Services as they do health services; that is, as an agency they can use when their social circumstances render them in need of help. The success of this approach will depend on joint working and cooperation in line with new codes of practice.

Health services may be of importance in treating and documenting injuries, offering advice on services and counselling available locally, and if legal action takes place making relevant records available.

There are various voluntary agencies and websites listed in the appendices that provide up-to-date information for victims of domestic violence.

Schools, like hospitals and GP surgeries, Social Services and police, should hold information on help for victims of domestic violence in the form of leaflets and phone contacts placed in an obvious place.

Points for practice

1   *Child protection* issues and procedures have to be followed in all cases where children might be experiencing abuse or violence. Social Services will intervene where there is a real risk of emotional or physical harm to the children, and they will sometimes use the threat of higher-tier intervention to encourage the mother to leave or take steps to remove a violent partner. In reality, many families live through repeated police and Social Services interventions, returning to patterns of behaviour and taking years to break the cycle, if indeed this is ever achieved. Other families exist with a level of violence that falls below anything that would lead to intervention and others make promises of change and action that satisfies authorities.

Police interventions are based on credible complaints and the willingness of witnesses to come forward. The witnesses do not have to be direct victims of the violence themselves to be considered credible. The police will make a decision as to whether to prosecute a perpetrator irrespective of the wishes of the victim. The victim may withdraw a statement, but the decision to prosecute lies with the police and the Crown Prosecution Service.

Where families are moving to escape domestic violence, care should be taken to ensure the continuity of education for the children as schools can remain a stable influence in their lives. Home/school support continues even when multi-agency intervention is in place, providing a continuity of care when circumstances improve.

2 *Support for children in school.* Any support for children within the school should be based on good contact with the parent victim and on trust and confidentiality, acknowledging the danger the family might be in. Domestic violence kills and injures people every week in the United Kingdom, and knowledge of the circumstances of a family should be restricted to those who need to know with a clear understanding of the consequences of talking openly. Even where there is no immediate danger from a perpetrator, many children are embarrassed and ashamed of their circumstances and will not access help if they feel it is not strictly in confidence. The confidentiality offered to childern in these circumstances should always be conditional on their safety.Where a staff member believes that child or others to be at serious risk of harm then these concerns must be acted upon.

3 *Personal safety.* As mentioned in the previous chapter, many home/school workers will visit homes and meet parents outside of school. Where domestic violence is an issue, then special steps need to be taken to ensure the safety of the worker. Risk assessments (see Appendix 2) should be undertaken regarding possible contact with the perpetrator at meetings, and home visits should not be attempted if there is any possibility of violence or intimidation. Senior management should be kept informed at all times during work with these families and should take steps to ensure the physical and emotional well-being of the worker. Working with families in these circumstances is particularly stressful. This should be taken into account and the worker should not seek to work single-handedly. Good multi-agency working is recommended and can successfully address many of these problems.

Summary

This chapter has attempted to illustrate the frequency with which incidences of domestic violence take place throughout the United Kingdom and the effect it has on children's emotional well-being and educational outcomes. The possible interventions through school have been described thoroughly. It has also shown how important it is for all school staff to have a better understanding and accommodation of how domestic violence can impact on children and their learning. Children's attendance at school is often the one stable factor in a disrupted and uncertain lifestyle while domestic violence persists or when a family seeks to escape. Making that environment safe and flexible to their needs and addressing those needs holistically may make a difference to their life-long educational and emotional outcomes.

〰️ Points for reflection

1 Unfortunately, domestic violence, in one form or another, is more common than is usually assumed. How do you think you would cope emotionally and practically with a situation in which domestic violence was involved?

2 Do you think you would be able to 'leave work at work' when you are having to work with a complex, emotionally draining case at school? How would you relax? Would you seek/expect supervision (special support talking with another more senior professional (usually) for coping with emotional work issues)?

3 Do you think that home/school support workers should get involved in such difficult and often complex situations? Why? Why not?

4 Reflect on how recent legislation could help schools and agencies support children affected by domestic violence.

5 How would you cope if you had to report a family to Social Services, knowing that it is likely a child may have to be removed (for their own safety) from the family home? Who would you go to for support?

📖 Further reading

Brecklin, L. (2002) 'The role of perpetrator alcohol use in the injury outcomes of intimate assaults', *Journal of Family Violence,* 17(3): 185–97.

Kershaw, C., Chivite-Matthews, N., Thomas, C. and Aust, R. (2001) *The 2001 British Crime Survey: First Results, England and Wales, 18/01.* London: HMSO. www.homeoffice.gov.uk/rds/pdfs/hosb1801.pdf

Mullender, A. (2004). 'Tackling Domestic Violence: Providing support for children who have witnessed domestic violence' Home Office Development and Practice Report online publication: www. renewal.net/Documents/RNET/Policy%20Guidance/Tackling domesticviolencechildren.pdf

Useful websites

Citizen Advice Bureau – www.citizensadvice.org.uk

National Domestic Violence Helpline – www.crimereduction.gov.uk/domesticviolence/domesticviolence40.htm

Refuges – www.womensaid.org.uk

Shelter – http://england.shelter.org.uk/home/index.cfm

3

Bereavement and Loss

This chapter will provide useful information for schools about how children and their families may experience difficulties coping with their feelings and emotions following a bereavement, or some type of loss. Topics examined will include:

- coping with a death in the family
- family break-up
- loss in the community
- life changes – moving home, school, etc.

Some of the confusion surrounding childhood grief and the way it presents in schools will be explored. Also, a number of ways will be suggested and illustrated through case studies to show how families can be supported by schools, enabling children to continue to attend and to view school as a safe haven even in the worst of crises. Adult fears around raising the issue of bereavement and grief as an aspect of Personal, Social and Health Education (PSHE) will be confronted, as well as how our own adult experiences of loss impede our ability to talk openly with children around this subject.

Bereavement and loss are complex and emotional issues and our own experiences can influence how issues are thought about or approached in work with the children. The following examples illustrate this point extremely clearly. In a 'Circle Time' session addressing issues of loss with Year 1 children, the home/school support worker raised the question, 'Who do you miss?' Children round the circle mentioned grandparents who had died, pets that had died, dads who no longer lived with them. Then one small traveller child said that she missed her mummy. The leader of the circle had seen the mother that morning and asked the child why she was missing her mother. 'Because I haven't seen her all day', was the reply.

This one small girl's experience of a long day at school away from her mother and her interpretation of the meaning of the question, 'Who do you miss?' exposes the whole area of childhood loss and bereavement laid bare of adult interpretations and socially acceptable meanings. The language we use to describe loss and bereavement, whether due to a death or divorce, a move from the area or a disappearance is fraught with pitfalls for a child. One father of a boy with learning difficulties, for example, found it impossible to say to his son that his mother had died. Instead, he would tell him she was in heaven, 'gone to sleep', or passed away. The boy became quite adamant in his contradiction of this, insisting that his mother was dead and buried in the ground, because after all he had seen this happen. Another boy who was told his father had died of a heart attack struggled with the meaning of the phrase and envisaged something inside his chest attacking his heart.

Every Child Matters

Types of loss
Although from an adult viewpoint bereavement is caused by the death of a relative or close personal friend, in reality, both children and adults suffer bereavement or more generally grieve for the loss of a person who has played a major part in their life. In that sense, grief may be felt following any of the following:

- death of a close friend or relative
- death of a pet
- separation and divorce
- an older sibling leaving home
- separation of families through fostering and adoption
- friendships lost through moving schools and areas
- serious illness in the family
- a disappearance.

 Case study: Zac, aged 9

Zac showed some serious deterioration in behaviour, angry outbursts and violence in school. It was quickly recognized that the deterioration began when his much older sister left home to live with her partner. There was no personal permanent loss involved, because the sister had remained within the local vicinity. However, it was realized that this sister had been effectively a surrogate mother to him since his earliest childhood as his own mother worked full-time, often in the evenings. Losing his sister, especially to someone else, was like losing his main carer to a stranger and it took him some months to settle down and get used to seeing her in a new, less maternal role.

To help with this situation, the home/school support worker spoke to Zac every week about how he was feeling and contacted his parents whenever there was something positive to celebrate. It was important to Zac that his good behaviour was recognized and rewarded. After two terms of trying, his school awarded him the prize for the pupil with the greatest improvement in his behaviour.

Points for practice

The school and Zac's parents could very easily have ignored the impact of his sister's move away from the home. However, in this case the school recognized that he was feeling a loss and then acknowledged that he was feeling angry and most probably jealous as well. By giving him the space and time to talk openly about his feelings on a regular basis over a period of time, Zac realized that:

- he could and should talk about his feelings (rather than act out his anger)
- adults were interested in how he was feeling
- his feelings were valued
- good behaviour also meant adults paid positive attention to you.

In this way, the school and parents were able to positively see Zac through his period of loss and also prevent his disengagement with school and learning.

There are no accurate statistics in this country for the numbers of children affected by the death of a parent or carer. The figures given by the Childhood Bereavement Network are between 4 and 7 per cent of 16-year-olds. The Winston's Wish organization estimates that 20,000 children suffer the death of a parent every year in this country. Similar figures can be calculated for children suffering the death of a sibling, but again there are no accurate statistics.

More than three quarters of children in secondary schools have suffered the loss of a close relative or friend during their lives, and if divorce and separation are added to the figures there are very few children who will not have suffered some form of loss by the time they reach their teenage years. Despite this, bereavement is rarely mentioned in many schools and addressing loss and grief as part of the curriculum is something that many teachers struggle with. Adults' own experiences of grieving may intrude and our adult-learned sensibilities about what can and cannot be said hamper simple straightforward language. Hence children learn that the pain of bereavement is something that it is not quite acceptable to talk about, and that bottling it up and getting on with life are desirable goals. Bereavement in adults is one of the most common causes of mental illness, so if we deal with it so badly, what chance is there for our children?

Be healthy and stay safe

The commonest form of bereavement is through the death of a close friend or relative when, regardless of the family connection, the significance to the child should be taken into consideration. An elderly aunt may not seem like a close connection, but where the child has had a special relationship with that person then the death may hit them badly.

Identification

Children finding it difficult to deal with issues around illness and death will exhibit symptoms that should alert staff, even if parents have not thought to inform school of an imminent bereavement. These may include:

- **crying** – from quiet weeping to full-blown inconsolable distress
- **withdrawal** – being sad and not wishing to play or work

- **anxiety** – worrying about surviving relatives, an awareness of others' grief and concern for them
- **practical worrying** – 'how will we manage without ...?'
- **clinging and attention**-seeking behaviour
- **mood changes** – sudden flashes of anger or weeping
- **inability to concentrate**
- **tiredness** – illness and bereavement lead to disrupted routines, nightmares and poor sleep patterns
- **loss of appetite**.

Where children present in this way, parents should be notified as soon as possible and asked if there could be a reason for this sudden change in behaviour.

There are certain groups within society that have been found to suffer more from bereavement. Social class plays a part, with death rates higher in areas of deprivation and unemployment where there are frequently more chronic healthcare needs. Children in special schools are more likely to suffer bereavement through the loss of a friend because of the complex health problems of young people with disabilities. Families where there are mental health or drug-related issues may be more generally affected with greater risks of suicide or accidental death.

Interventions

Practical considerations around the care of children should be addressed particularly where the deceased was a main carer. If there is a welfare problem, the death of a main carer may lead to children being neglected or inadequately protected, particularly if the remaining carer is badly affected themselves. School provides a consistent point of contact and may be the first place where concerns are raised. A home/school worker can make contact in the early stages of bereavement offering sympathy and practical help, and alerting the family to the needs of the children. This can be done sensitively, but should not be delayed where there are concerns about any child's well-being. Where school child protection procedures become necessary, the criteria for referral should be that used for all child protection concerns, i.e. the child's physical, emotional and social well-being should be assessed regardless of the excuses for these concerns. Bereavement and other family crises should not be excuses for abuse or neglect. In one case a child of four was being left to fend for herself because her carer's mental health was so badly affected by the death of her partner. It was necessary for this child to spend time in respite foster care until her family was once more able to care for her.

To summarize:

- Child welfare should be carefully considered: are the children being fed, clothed properly, kept safe from harm?
- Where families have a history of child protection concerns due to other issues, a bereavement may make matters worse.
- Early, sensitively offered help will often prevent crises in care by helping families to focus on the needs of the children in practical ways.
- Criteria outlined in other chapters in this book, e.g. Chapter 5 on neglect poverty, will help workers to judge where child protection issues might arise.

Most importantly:

- The school Child Protection Officer and/or the home/school support worker's line manager or supervisor should be kept informed of all concerns.
- Decisions should be taken regarding any child protection issues in line with the school's child protection policy.

Enjoy and achieve: make a positive contribution

Bereavement impacts enormously on a child's ability to function in school and can affect concentration, academic progress and emotional well-being. The nature of the bereavement will play a large part in how the child and the wider family react. For the purpose of this discussion, bereavement will be separated into two main areas:

1 Expected death through illness.
2 Unexpected death as a result of accident, injury, suicide or sudden illness.

1 *Expected death through illness.* Where a death is expected or at least predicted in some way, there is time to help prepare a child for what is going to happen. The child will be coming regularly to school and, depending on how much they have been told of the illness, there may be a need to offer support during school time. One very common situation arising for staff within schools is the reluctance of parents to tell children or the school that such a situation exists. In many cases, the first person to tell a member of staff of the serious illness of a close relative is the child himself. Given that they will frequently have a poor or distorted understanding of the situation, it then becomes necessary to contact parents and ask if there is anything we can do or any help we can offer to support the child. The parent can sometimes be surprised by the child's understanding and knowledge of the situation. Parents comment that they did not think the child was aware of what was going on or had not been told it was serious. Coaching parents and encouraging them to communicate with their children is important at any stage of the process. Left to their own imagination, children will imagine the worst and their worst may be far more frightening than reality.

Points for practice

Again, as in the previous examples, it is acknowledging and then acting on information provided that can make a real difference to the way a child may feel about how they can or should cope with a loss or bereavement. To have a school adult listen and then support them can really be very positive for children. They may also be very relieved that someone else is able to tell their parent(s)/carer how they are feeling or (not) coping with a situation. Many adults may feel that it is insensitive to disturb a family at such a time, but it is important that as a professional you are firstly responsible for the health and well-being of the children. If this is at risk then it is right to alert the parent(s)/carers as soon as possible of your concerns, obviously as sensitively and supportively as anyone can in such a situation.

2 *Unexpected death as a result of accident, injury, suicide or sudden illness*. This can take many forms and will most probably affect every school and every teacher at some stage in her career. Being aware of the possibility of sudden deaths within a community goes some way to helping a school cope when an event happens, and a contingency plan should exist together with some regular staff training. Some schools have a policy and procedure already in place so that if and when an incident occurs, the practicalities have already been carefully considered. In this case, the list of duties only need to be followed and clear thinking (often when this is very difficult) is not imperative to ensure a situation is dealt with thoroughly and appropriately.

Sudden deaths can be due to any of the following:

- sudden illness, heart attack, stroke, etc.
- accidental death – road traffic, workplace, holiday, domestic
- drug- or alcohol-related accidental overdoses
- suicide
- violent non-accidental death – murder or manslaughter as a result of crime
- death by any of these causes of a member of the school community: teacher, child, parent, support staff member.

In any of these situations, there are issues for children to deal with around shock, trauma, understanding and accepting the fact of the death and dealing with the fear and anxiety associated with the event. Just as adults are traumatized by such an incident, so too are children, although their ways of expressing that trauma are limited by their understanding (see Appendix 4).

Interventions

In-school support for children

Within a school, there are ways in which bereavement can be sensitively handled and comfort given. Some of these ways are simple and effective and do not involve a great outlay of time or effort on the part of staff.

1 The most important response to bereavement is **communication**. It is vital to keep channels of communication open and to give opportunities for children to talk. It is also important that all involved members of staff are informed that a child needs careful consideration during the grieving process. A supply teacher coming in needs to know that a child is grieving and might need special attention. Midday meal supervisors and teaching assistants may notice a child is upset or withdrawn and need to know why and what to do. Therefore, by informing all members of staff, the child is cared for throughout the day. Designated members of staff with appropriate training should be known to children who are bereaved and opportunities can then be given to speak to them on request.

2 Allow for **changes in behaviour, concentration and emotions**. Give a child 'time out' if necessary and be flexible with rules. A bereaved child might need to be inside during break times or may need to leave lessons suddenly when feelings become too much to handle within a classroom setting. They may need extra encouragement, time alone and space to think.

3 **Remember that we do not 'get over' or 'recover from'** a bereavement. Adults and children learn to cope with their loss and deal with the changes it brings. Introducing ways to remember the person, such as a memories box or a wall display for photographs and poems, allows a child to demonstrate grief physically. Other methods of remembering include special books, flowers, pictures, garden spaces, prayers and quiet areas. These areas can be renewed and revisited throughout the year to acknowledge the continuing nature of bereavement. It is too often unacknowledged how important it is to physically and visually demonstrate grief; for a child who can find it extremely difficult to express his feelings using language, much comfort can be gained from physically or visually demonstrating their love and sense of loss.

Points for practice

With attendance and truancy being a very important issue in schools currently, it is important to remember that for certain children it is vital for their emotional and mental well-being for them to visit a grave or a specific area on a particular day, such as a dead mother's birthday. On such an occasion, compassionate dispensation for one day may well prevent longer-term issues from developing.

4 It is important that **bereavement is addressed** with all the children, probably most effectively through PSHE lessons, circle time and assemblies. Children who are prepared with the language and skills to talk about dying cope better when it happens.
5 **Involve the whole community** in talking about bereavement and loss. Parents and carers, extended families and local religious leaders can all play a part in remembering and celebrating a life that was valued and loved.
6 Include **books and stories** about bereavement in your school library.
7 Consider **multicultural aspects of the community** and how different faiths and cultural groups grieve.

Points for practice

Books, stories and talks by local religious leaders and volunteer groups can all play a significant role for adults and children in a school community learning how different cultures cope and manage bereavement and loss. It is very important to try to talk about these issues when no one is dealing with very 'raw' feelings of loss. When this is possible, children can then feel comfortable to ask questions which are significant for them, and perhaps are worrying them, but in a more emotional situation would not feel able to ask. Stories and books can also demonstrate how other children and adults have learnt to cope with their feelings of loss. Again, they can provide a positive way of answering sensitive but very real queries children may have.

Supporting parent/carers

Opening channels of communication with parents suffering bereavement is always a challenge. Families may be busy in the midst of organizing funerals and dealing with the practicalities of the death. They may be traumatized by a sudden death and struggling to cope themselves. Telephoning and asking how they are and offering support is rarely met with anything but gratitude. It can be very supportive to know that the school your child attends is willing to show and demonstrate their concern for all the family. Some people's cultural tendency is to step back from a family when someone has died and to avoid contact or conversation. However, this can often feel very isolating for a family and especially for the children.

Attending funerals as a home/school support worker is a natural part of family support. Where you have known and worked with a parent, the home/school support worker's presence is an extension and continuation of concern and support. Choosing to attend a funeral will depend on the nature of your contact with the family and the family member who has died. Your judgement will tell you when this is appropriate.

Some basic advice to parents and carers in helping children to cope with a death could include:

- talking honestly and at the child's level about the death, what happened and why
- keeping in touch with school and informing school of the situation in the home
- explaining about the funeral and trying to include the child in decisions about music, readings, etc.
- communicating your feelings and reassuring the child that you are sad, but can still care for them
- being aware that children may have a distorted idea of cause and effect and feel in some way to blame for the death, particularly a sudden or violent death. Reassure them that they are not to blame
- being aware that children will 'forget' and have fun and laugh for a while and then remember and feel sad again. Reassure them that fun and laughter are all right and they should not feel guilty
- talking to them about how they are feeling, particularly if they are not sleeping or have little appetite
- allowing them the opportunity to determine how they would like to be involved in the funeral or how they would like to say 'goodbye' to the deceased
- being ready to seek help if you feel you are not coping
- being ready to seek help if you feel the children are not coping.

Other forms of bereavement
Divorce and Separation
In the majority of school communities, many children are in families that do not include both of their natural parents. Divorce and separation is becoming a much more common issue within our society. Family break-ups unfortunately happen very frequently now and, as a result, schools give little real attention to them. This chapter is focusing on the concerns connected with the immediate impact of loss. Undoubtedly when parents divorce or separate, loss is a large part of the trauma for children. Separation causes loss of two kinds: firstly the loss of a lifestyle and of a familiar routine, and, secondly, the actual physical separation from someone the child loves and is used to. The symptoms this causes are similar to those caused by a death, but with the added confusion of uncertainty about the future role of the absent person. Dealing with separation is often more difficult than bereavement, as the parents can be at odds and behaving in ways that ignore the best interests of the children.

Home/school support workers have to tread considerately and keeping the welfare and well-being of the children foremost in conversations with parents helps to maintain a neutral stance, i.e. 'I take no side in arguments between parents; I represent what is best for the child or children'.

Disappearance

This topic has been included in this chapter as it is becoming more of an issue in recent years. In such cases, a parent/sibling/relative will go missing and children are left knowing nothing – whether they are alive or dead or whether they love them or not! Educational Psychology (EP) services and Child and Adolescent Mental Health Services (CAMHS) can play a significant role in these very difficult cases, but where the wider school community is concerned, honesty has proven to be the best course of action, with senior staff explaining in appropriately clear language that a person has gone away somewhere and not told anyone else. Staff need to say that when the adults understand what has happened they will tell the children. Meanwhile, understanding and support for the children of a parent who has disappeared can follow the same lines as for bereaved children. As with suicide and divorce, children will feel responsible and guilty and should be reassured that it is not their fault. Acknowledging and affirming the validity of feelings allows a child to feel that they are not to blame and that their reactions are normal given the circumstances.

Achieve economic well-being

The death of a main breadwinner will seriously affect the economic well-being of a family and can lead to many difficult problems. Home/school support workers can play a significant role in offering financial advice and support, sorting benefits and finding charitable funding if necessary. This help can be accessed through Citizen's Advice Bureaux, benefits agencies and solicitors. A home/school support worker can ensure that a family is aware that this help is available and can be accessed should they need it.

Multi-agency working

Parents and carers in these situations are often grateful for support and advice with children. There are several good organizations that support children who have been bereaved: notably, Winston's Wish (www.winstonswish.org.uk), the Childhood Bereavement Network (www.childhoodbereavementnetwork.org.uk) and the BBC relationships site which has good links to other organizations. Locally, the Child and Adolescent Mental Health Services (CAMHS) (accessed through school or GP surgeries) and the Educational Psychology team are accessible and will offer bereavement support.

Where the death has been due to criminal violence, Victim Support (www.victim.support.org.uk) may offer advice and the police will have access to counselling services.

Personal and staff support

Within any school, staff members will also have suffered bereavements and our capacity to cope with emotionally draining situations will be affected by our own experiences. It is important to provide adequate supervision and support for workers engaged in working with bereaved families.

Whole staff training and support around bereavement should take place regularly and staff should also have access to counselling where relevant.

Children's reactions

It should be borne in mind that children have not learned appropriate and acceptable reactions to death. Where children have suffered bereavement, other children within the school may find themselves reacting in sympathy, even when they did not know the deceased. The most straightforward way to deal with this seems to be to reassure them that this is a natural reaction and that doing something practical and supportive for the bereaved children will help them feel better. Bereaved children often feel reassured by the continuing normality of school and this can help families enormously, particularly where they are confident their child will be looked after in school. It is not always necessary to send a child home if they are crying. They should feel that crying in school is acceptable.

Transitions and examinations

Children who are bereaved will need extra help to cope with changes and challenges. Practical help may be needed to support bereaved families through their child's examinations or through transition: everything from transport to filling in forms and making choices may prove difficult at these times. Where a child is moving to secondary school or between primary schools, then an adult who can visit both schools can provide invaluable support.

Points for practice

Each individual case you come across as a home/school support worker will prove different and will be difficult for you in many different ways. The following case studies each have their own set of problems with pointers for understanding and good practice. They have been chosen to show the range of situations that can involve children and bereavement. They aim to illustrate the types of intervention required and the often inadequate ways in which we deal with loss.

 Case study: Three teenage boys involved in an accident

In an inner-city community served by a primary school with several hundred children, an accident occurred over the school holiday involving three teenagers who had borrowed a car. Two were killed and one was critically injured when the car hit a lorry and crashed into a ditch. The mother of one of the dead teenagers was a teaching assistant at the primary school, the other teenager killed had two younger brothers in the school and the injured boy had several cousins there. All three boys were well-known locally and had previously attended the primary school.

Points for practice

Following the accident, the head teacher called an assembly and explained simply and factually what had happened and told the children who had died. The two younger brothers of the dead boy were not in school that day. The children were asked to pray if they felt able and told that they could ask to speak to a teaching assistant, pastoral support worker or teacher if they were very upset during the day. Times were set aside in the classrooms for this and several children were visibly upset.

The school home/school worker contacted the family with children in the school to ask about funeral arrangements and offer support. The families invited her to attend the funerals. In the following weeks, she helped the families to access bereavement counselling for the children in school. Several lunchtime drop-ins were arranged for children wishing to access support or express their grief in the next few months. Consideration was given to long-term support for those closely affected.

 Case study: Rebecca, aged 11

> Rebecca's parents separated and she spent part of the week with her father and the rest of the time with her mother. Her mother worked long hours and Rebecca cared for herself most of the time. If she wasn't working, Rebecca's mother would go out without her. Rebecca's grandmother, Sheila, lived close by and provided a much-needed refuge for Rebecca. With Sheila, Rebecca was cared for and felt safe and loved. Sadly Sheila died suddenly of a heart attack and Rebecca was left bereft. The family knew they were close, but no one fully realized how much Rebecca had depended on her grandmother. Her behaviour in school suddenly became angry and unpredictable and she was unable to work.

Points for practice

To help Rebecca, the home/school support worker spoke at length with her mother about her involvement in Sheila's funeral. In this way, Rebecca was able to read a poem and lay her own wreath. With the home/school worker's help, she made a box of memories and planted a pot of bulbs. Sheila had been very religious, but Rebecca said she wasn't able to believe in God because she felt so bad about losing her gran. Instead, she was encouraged to think about her happy memories and how proud her grandmother was of her. Eventually, she did make a prayer for Sheila.

In school, she was given a time-out card and staff and pupils were reminded regularly that she would need support. A transition plan was organized with her secondary school to help them understand Rebecca's home circumstances and needs. The home/school worker kept Rebecca's mother and father informed of all these arrangements and encouraged them to take an active part in supporting their daughter. Both mother and daughter agreed to access bereavement counselling.

Case study: Tara, aged 7

Tara's mother was expecting a baby and had told Tara. Scans had shown that the baby was a girl and Tara was very excited. At 22 weeks, her mother was involved in a car accident and lost the baby. Although the family told Tara straight away, her mother was very traumatized by the miscarriage and Tara was left worried about her mother and grieving for the sister she had hoped for. In school, she became tearful and clingy with members of staff, especially her teaching assistant.

Points for practice

The home/school support worker contacted Tara's family, but Tara's mother was very reluctant to engage and stated that she did not need any counselling. She was prepared to come into school to talk about Tara's behaviour since the accident. In an interview with the home/school worker, she said that Tara's behaviour at home was very difficult and she was refusing to sleep without her mother being in the room with her. She agreed to the school accessing play therapy for Tara and began coming into school herself regularly to speak with the home/school worker. Eventually, she agreed to some counselling which she accessed through her GP.

 Case study: Carla, aged 13

Carla is the youngest daughter of a father who is in his sixties. Her father suffers from heart disease and emphysema. When she was 13, an older brother from her father's previous marriage committed suicide by hanging himself. Carla suffered nightmares and anxiety following this, especially as her father was traumatized and was ill after the death. As her older brother had suffered from mental illness, Carla also began to fear that she too would become ill in this way. Carla's mother who has a good relationship with the school and particularly the home/school worker sought help for Carla through the school.

Points for practice

Carla was offered bereavement counselling through a local primary intervention project run jointly with Social Services and the Child and Adolescent Mental Health Services. She attended several group sessions with other children her own age and found that this 'helped me to learn how to talk about things openly. I stopped having terrible nightmares. I felt more in control'.

Carla's father and mother also talked about accessing counselling through their GP. Carla's father found he couldn't speak to 'strangers' about his problems, but did come and speak to the home/school support worker on several occasions.

Case study: Stephen, Joel and Martin, aged 16

Stephen, Joel and Martin had been friends since primary school. They were inseparable and planned to go to college together after completing their exams. At 16, Joel, who suffered badly from asthma, died after an acute attack. Stephen and Martin were badly affected and found the following months leading up to their exams especially difficult. Joel's family were supported through counselling, but little help was offered to Stephen and Martin. Their secondary school was informed by Martin's mother that he was very depressed and had talked to his girlfriend about killing himself.

Points for practice

The pastoral support worker (home/school worker) spoke to both the boys and offered them counselling for bereavement in school. Both boys agreed, as long as they could attend together. Following their experience, they set up a bereavement support group in their school when they entered sixth form the following term. The pastoral support worker supported them in this and accessed advice for them through the Educational Psychology service.

 Summary

To conclude, we have highlighted in this chapter, the inevitability of bereavement and loss as issues that will directly impact on children's ability to learn. It is hoped that these final case studies illustrate the wide range of loss and bereavement children and young people can experience at any time throughout their school life. How they cope and therefore how they manage to remain positively engaged with education and learning is vital. By ensuring the appropriate support and understanding is available, the school community can often provide the stability they need at such a vulnerable time.

 Points for reflection

1 Consider carefully how you have coped with bereavement and loss yourself in the past. Reflect on why you think you managed by reacting in a certain manner and how your loss affected you in the short and long term. Remember, loss and bereavement may not always be felt only when someone dies, but can include many kinds of transitions and changes throughout your life.
2 How do you think you will be able to support a child and their family when a close family member dies?

(Continued)

(Continued)

3   Why do you think that a transition, such as the move to secondary school, can be so traumatic for some children? How would you try to support children moving from primary to secondary school? Would you try to involve the whole school and/or outside agencies?

4   Think carefully about where you could find helpful information about how other cultures and faiths cope and deal with bereavement and loss.

 Further reading

Childhood Bereavement Network (2006) *A Guide to Developing Good Practice in Childhood Bereavement Services.* London: National Children's Bureau.

Job, N. and Frances, G. (2004) *Childhood Bereavement.* London: National Children's Bureau.

McAuliffe, A-M., Linsey, A. and Fowler, J. (2006) *Childcare Act 2006.* London: National Children's Bureau.

Ribbens McCarthy, J.R. with Jessop, J. (2005) *Young People, Bereavement and Loss: Disruptive transitions?* London: National Children's Bureau.

 Useful websites

Childhood Bereavement Network – www.childhoodbereavementnetwork.org.uk has a very good list of support materials and books for all children and young people and school staff at: www.childhoodbereavementnetwork.org.uk/publications_suggested Reading.htm

Child Bereavement Trust also has a list of very useful reading and storybooks for children and young people. They can be viewed at: www.childbereavement.org.uk/resources/reading_children.php

Circle Time – www.circle-time.co.uk/site/home

Citizen's Advice Bureau – www.citizensadvice.org.uk

Winston's Wish – www.winstonswish.org.uk

Special Educational Needs: Learning Difficulties

This chapter will provide guidance about the variety of interventions and agency support that parents and carers of children with Special Educational Needs (SEN) may need to enable them to access the help, advice and support they require. It will focus on how the home/school support worker can be utilized by a school to help parents and carers with these issues. It will describe how home/school support workers can help children deal with social and emotional problems or with a change in routine, usefully sharing knowledge and skills with other professionals.

Another term that schools and other professionals use to describe need is 'Additional Education Need' (AEN). This is a term used to describe any type of need a learner may be experiencing. As you can see from Figure 4.1, Special Educational Needs (SEN) is just one issue included within the framework for additional educational needs, and a learner does not have to have a special educational need to have additional educational needs.

This chapter is focusing on the learning needs of children and young people and thus will concentrate on issues relating to a child's special educational needs only.

The Special Educational Needs Code of Practice defines special educational needs in the following way:

> Children have special educational needs if they have a learning difficulty which calls for special educational provision to be made for them. (DfES, 2001: 6)

It describes a 'learning difficulty' and provides explanations of the fundamental principles. Importantly, it recognizes that there is a wide spectrum of special educational needs that may be interrelated, but that there are four identified specific areas of need:

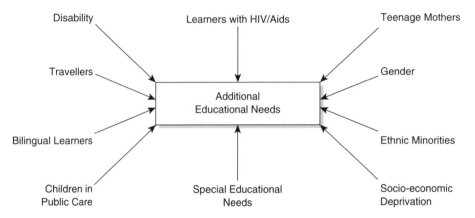

Figure 4.1   Reasons why learners may have Additional Educational Needs (AEN)

1   communication and interaction
2   cognition and learning
3   behaviour, emotional and social development
4   sensory and/or physical impairment.

The SEN Code of Practice (DfES, 2001, 1:33) states that 'all schools should admit pupils with already identified special educational needs, as well as identifying and providing for pupils not previously identified as having SEN.' Furthermore, it goes on to say: 'There is a clear expectation within the Education Act 1996 that pupils with statements of special educational needs will be included in mainstream schools' (1:35).

There is now a clear expectation that schools will make provision for children who have widely different educational needs with and without Statements of Educational Needs. There is also an expectation that provision should be a natural part of the mainstream school process and that all pupils will benefit from the wider experience of inclusion and the expertise it encourages in staff. It is not unusual for staff members to be trained in dealing with Autistic Spectrum Disorders (ASD), cerebral palsy, blindness and Down's syndrome. The skills gained in these fields may then be transferred to other areas to the benefit of the whole school.

Difficulties arise with this approach when the SEN of the pupil involves behavioural difficulties that might pose a threat to the education or well-being of the other pupils. There may also be instances where the difficulties are so profound that the child cannot achieve in a mainstream setting and needs more specialist provision. Challenges also occur when children may have difficulties which are new to the school. In these circumstances, there can be a delay in implementing provision due to lack of training and equipment and this may need additional support. Local authorities should do all they can to support schools to support the children with special educational needs in the most appropriate manner, providing the relevant training.

The 'Index for Inclusion' (CSIE, 2002, Figure 1.3) makes it clear that 'inclusion' is not just about children with identified special educational needs. Inclusion should be about 'reducing barriers to learning and participation for all students, not only those with impairments or those who are categorized as "having special educational needs"'.

Building on this, the SEN Code of Practice (DfES, 2001) dedicates a whole section to the role of parents and the partnership required to understand fully the needs of a child. It states that 'professionals should: draw on parental knowledge and expertise in relation to their child and recognize the personal and emotional investment of parents and be aware of their feelings' (DfES, 2001, 2:7). Further, to this there are clear rights under law regarding a parent's authority and responsibility (Children's Act 1989) and the rights of the child to an inclusive mainstream education (Education Act 1996).

For the purposes of this chapter, 'special educational needs' is interpreted to mean any learning difficulty a child might experience, no matter how small or how temporary. The same problems and worries for parents occur whether the child is newly diagnosed with a distinct disorder, or has lived with a learning difficulty all of their life. For these parents, education is a challenge above and beyond the usual routine of supporting and liaising with school.

Every Child Matters

The following sections of this chapter illustrate through examples and case studies how children with special educational needs and their families can be effectively supported by home/school support workers.

As Tutt and Barthorpe (2006:12) state: 'Every child must matter and every child must feel equally valued.' For many children with special educational needs, a holistic 'child' approach is not enough to enable them to maximize their potential. They and their family will require support in various forms and it is the home/school support worker, working closely with the SEN team who can facilitate the agencies to ensure the social and health needs of the whole family are met. With these issues supported, the child is more able to focus on their learning and educational progress.

Supporting parents: being healthy and being safe

For a parent with a child who has learning difficulties, the process of assessing and defining that child's needs may be long and complex. It may include multi-agency input involving many assessments and appointments that will be reviewed and changed as the child develops. Understanding and admitting to a child's needs may be a difficult process in itself, with a realization that a child is going to need different and/or additional support and is not able to cope with school in the same way as most of his peers. Depending on the severity and nature of the learning difficulty, parents may or may not have come to terms with it. Some parents are resistant to labelling a child with a specific disorder, doing all they can to avoid special treatment, while others will follow any lead to access whatever help is available and insist on some form of named diagnosis. Both reactions must be respected and parent opinions valued. Parents have watched their children grow and develop and care for them day and night. They are usually right about their needs and requirements.

The support and help that a home/school support worker can provide should complement that of the SENCO and other members of the teaching staff. Within a school team, the SENCO is the designated person who manages the needs of SEN children with a team of specialist teaching assistants (TA) working with all of the class teachers. Pastoral care and liaison with families should be an integral part of that team work. Children with special needs may also present with any of the problems discussed in other chapters. Strong team support for families ensures that any difficulties are dealt with early on; prevention is always preferable.

Children with SEN are often more vulnerable within the school setting to peer problems, isolation, bullying, access and environment difficulties. In other words, depending on the nature of their needs, they may require special provision to deal with any aspect of the school environment. A child with mobility problems may have difficulties with crowded corridors and stairways, even if they normally manage to move around well out of school. One child with a growth deficiency found secondary transition particularly difficult with the prospect of crowds of much larger children, as well as their general reaction to his size. The pastoral support of such children should involve the prediction of these kinds of problems through good communication with the children and their families. Providing opportunities for children to voice their concerns and needs is good practice and anticipates difficulties that may easily be overcome. Furthermore, involving peer support through schemes like circle of friends, peer mentoring and buddying can increase confidence and involvement in school.

Consideration of health and safety for these children should extend to all areas of schooling including travel and out-of-school activities. Good communication with families is vital for this. A child may be failing to take up extracurricular opportunities because parents cannot guarantee their safety and creative solutions may be possible to allow the child to fully participate.

A home/school worker can spend time listening to the views and concerns of the parents and child, and help provide additional information, and a different level and kind of support to that of a school and its teaching staff. The home/school worker can also support the parents at meetings, visit other schools and establishments with the family, thus helping to make sure they have all the information they require to make informed decisions.

This type of family support ensures that the parents and the child with special educational needs are supported through the assessment process in a fair and open way. Whether this eventually means a move to another school or additional support in the current establishment, it demonstrates to parents that their views (and that of their child) are valued and listened to by the school.

 Case study: Ryan, aged 12

Ryan is the youngest of three brothers. His mother Charlotte is now single and has brought up her children alone since Ryan was one year old. Ryan has both physical and behavioural difficulties. He is very large for his age and clumsy, finding running and climbing difficult. Since starting school, he has found relationships with other children difficult and now has a diagnosis of Asperger's syndrome. Throughout his schooling, Charlotte has been supported by her home/school support worker, Mary. This worker has accompanied Charlotte to meetings, helped Ryan to express his opinions and wishes about his education provision and listened to Charlotte when she has been anxious and depressed about Ryan's future. She also encouraged Charlotte to claim carer's allowance for Ryan and helped her to fill in the forms. Ryan's oldest brother, though not as severely affected, is also diagnosed with an autistic spectrum disorder. As Ryan's transition to secondary school approached, Mary accompanied Charlotte on visits to potential schools for Ryan. Charlotte and Ryan eventually chose a secondary school with a specialist unit for children with autistic spectrum disorders. Charlotte is now studying for a degree and Ryan is successfully attending secondary school and making new friends.

Points for practice

Firstly, this home/school support worker prevented Charlotte from becoming isolated and from feeling alone when having to make important education choices for her children. The support worker also helped Charlotte during the transition process to secondary school by accompanying her to other schools and providing information. Throughout this process, the support worker ensured Ryan's views and concerns were taken into consideration as well. Additionally, the worker informed Charlotte that she may be able to receive financial aid for Ryan and provided practical support.

In this way, the support worker provided a level of help that a school teaching staff member would not be able to give. With discussion and collaboration between the school and support worker, Ryan achieved a successful transition into secondary school. Charlotte also found encouragement and confidence in her own abilities by being given practical, consistent advice and input. Without this regular and consistent help, the outcomes for Ryan and Charlotte could have been very different.

Enjoy and achieve and making a positive contribution

If inclusion is to be effective for children with special educational needs, then the professionals around them should have high expectations of them and support them, as with any other child, in taking part in all school activities. Giving children with special educational needs opportunities to contribute to school councils, student newspapers and debates on school issues should be actively encouraged, just as much as ensuring they can take part in trips or school performances. They should also be allowed to develop their own individual talents, and those talents should be celebrated by the school. One such example of a school recognizing the needs and talents of a child is given below.

Case study: Shauna, aged 9

Shauna has cerebral palsy and is partially sighted. She has a great deal of help in school with equipment and therapy. School works closely with Shauna's mother Meg, especially through Julie, the home/school support worker. Recently, Meg mentioned to Julie that Shauna is a strong swimmer and has won several certificates with her local club. Julie suggested that she might like to show them at the school certificate assembly and consulted with Shauna about this. Shauna is very shy and was reluctant, but she agreed so long as her best friend could stand up with her. The school has arranged a swimming gala and Shauna is keen to take part. Her year group is involved in the planning and the experience has improved Shauna's confidence and self-esteem.

Points for practice

It was important to recognize Shauna as an individual with her own special talents, but also to understand that she is a shy person who needs support to stand up before the school. The home/school support worker in these cases needs to work slowly and ensure that Shauna's feelings are respected. Good communication with Shauna's mother and contact on a casual basis, daily greeting at the school gate, etc. allows parents to mention things in a relaxed way, rather than waiting for an official opportunity.

For some children, inclusion may involve withdrawal from their mainstream classes for a few hours, or to receive special provision within classrooms. For others, different provisions or teaching strategies and interventions will need to be implemented. To enable a child with an autistic spectrum disorder to achieve as well as he can, for example, he may need to participate only for part of his school day in big group activities, finding small groups and quiet spaces more conducive to his needs. Also, it is important to remember that where there are behavioural difficulties, parental solutions are often extremely effective, being based on a deeper understanding of the child and long practice. Talking regularly with parents when such difficulties arise may make all the difference.

Children with special educational needs can achieve highly in mainstream schools when the team of professionals and agencies listen to and respect the views of parents and the children themselves. Each child must be treated as an individual, and intervention and strategies put in place by a school need to be flexible and creative. If they are achieving, all children, whatever their needs or disability, can see that they are equally valued and respected as members of the school community.

Achieve economic well-being

Having a child with a special educational need can mean that there are additional costs a family will have to try to afford. These can be expensive and prohibitive, involving equipment and treatment for the child, and/or loss of earnings for the parents. Accessing grants and benefits may present problems for parents under pressure and where the difficulties are not physical or obvious, families may never have received any help, being unaware that they are eligible.

Home/school support should enable parents to come and ask for help, but many things stand in the way of that. In practice, difficulties become apparent when parents are asked to pay for trips or children come to school lacking equipment or uniform. Some families struggle for years and never complain. Benefits like Disability Living Allowance and additional transport benefits can make a big difference to parents on low incomes. Home/school support workers can hold details of these and make them available to parents, who may then require help to fill in quite detailed and complicated forms.

Other help available for families may be through local charities or national help groups supporting families with specific problems. Most of these non-statutory agencies are more than willing to be approached by the families themselves or by the home/school worker.

Multi-agency working

With children with special educational needs, multi-agency working often requires liaison with the local health authority and the school nurse teams. These agencies can frequently be extremely helpful, providing vital support for children with special educational needs. Other useful agencies to contact will depend upon the needs of each child, but will most probably include providers of specialist equipment, speech and language and occupational therapists, clinics and specialist social workers.

Where a child's disability has been catered for within school for many years, outside agencies that deal regularly with children as they grow may provide insight into the changing needs of children as they approach puberty and transition.

 Case study: Smila, aged 10

Smila has diabetes and began her puberty early in Year 5. Vida, her mother, spoke with the home/school support worker who she was comfortable working with and they arranged for Smila to talk with the school nurse. She also spoke to her specialist diabetes nurse. Her local diabetes support group arranged for her to speak to a group of older girls about the problems and solutions they had experienced.

Points for practice
There is considerable support available for children with diabetes, mostly organized into child-centred activities and groups. Home/school support workers can learn a great deal from parents like Vida who knew how to access help

for her daughter. They can then pass this information on to other parents or arrange networking for them. Most parents are only too willing to help others in the same situation.

Smila's diabetes was under control but her changing body presented new challenges for her, especially as she was so young. Children with learning and medical conditions experience the same difficulties growing up as their peers, complicated by their special problems. Provision and support for these children should be reviewed periodically and opportunities made for parents and children to express concerns.

The following two case studies illustrate how a home/school support worker may be required to help children and families while working with different agencies. They all also demonstrate that the home/school worker ensures he encourages the families, with the necessary support, to make changes for themselves. Families must be empowered to make decisions for themselves whenever possible, unless of course the children are at risk, if decisive action is not taken by others outside of the family.

 Case study: Lucy, aged 7, and Boris, aged 4

Andy and Fatima have two children both with global delay and learning difficulties. Boris who is four is more severely affected and has a place at a special school. Lucy attends mainstream school and is seven. She is very small for her age and delayed in most areas of her learning. She has the support of a teaching assistant for most of the week, and works with her age group for part of the week and with the reception class for some afternoons. Her programme of support is carefully tailored to her educational needs.

Andy and Fatima have received help from Social Services for several years. Lucy is often late for school and often presents as neglected and hungry. Sam, the school home/school support worker, visits the family regularly. He encourages better attendance in school and good presentation and liaises with Social Services when there are difficulties. He supports Andy and Fatima at meetings, ensuring they understand the implications of what is said and helping them to put across their own point of view. He has a difficult job encouraging them to better parenting and not providing that care for them, so when Lucy is hungry in school, he visits to find out if there is a problem with shopping or money and asks why Lucy is not eating at home. Andy and Fatima have problems parenting their children and Sam has arranged for them to attend a parenting course in school.

Points for practice

The case study described here provides a crucial example of an important element of the role of the home/school support worker. It is vital that a support worker *does not* 'do' everything or even 'some' things for parents. It is the worker's role to provide information, training and/or support to enable parents to achieve what they want to, and arrive at decisions with the best interest of their child/ren in mind. This can be extremely powerful for families and especially for children who, perhaps for the first time, can see their parent(s) showing a positive interest in their general well-being and/or education. As the example also illustrates, this process frequently requires long-term intervention, with multi-agency input. Without Sam's ongoing support, Lucy and Boris may well have been removed from their family home, because Sam ensured:

- he attended Social Services meetings to help Andy and Fatima voice their views and feelings
- he kept a regular eye on the home and general well-being of the children
- the parents were offered and encouraged to attend further parenting workshops, etc.

Hence, while the school is providing an individual programme to meet Lucy's learning needs, the home/school support worker is trying to ensure the home environment continues to be a positive one, giving Lucy the best opportunity to access her education.

 Case study: Petros, aged 10, and Carlo, aged 7

Petros and Carlo both have learning difficulties. Petros is an intelligent 10-year-old with Asperger's syndrome and a serious bowel condition. He is overweight and eats compulsively; then he will soil himself. He has never had bowel control. Carlo has attention deficit hyperactivity disorder (ADHD) and significant learning difficulties. He has a Statement of Educational Needs and a supportive programme of learning in place at school. Even so, his behaviour at home and in school is challenging. Petros and Carlo's parents both work full-time and also care for the boys' grandmother who has dementia.

Sue, the home/school support worker, has supported the family since Carlo started school. She set up a meeting with the school nurse and the bowel clinic nurse who has been seeing Petros. The clinic nurse was able to explain Petros' condition to Sue and she was then able to explain it better to Petros, who is very literal and presumed it was his fault for eating the wrong food.

Petros was very reluctant to attend hospital appointments or receive treatment, but with Sue's help and explanations and the support of the school nurse, he was able to undergo treatment once he understood what was going to happen. His treatment was successful and he returned to school pleased and more confident.

Sue also helped the boys' mother to access carers' allowance and some respite care. Sue accompanied her at her request to secondary schools for Petros and helped explain his condition and ASD to his Year 7 tutor. Sue

(Continued)

(Continued)

maintained her support for the family for several years while Carlo progressed through school, helping whenever there were difficulties both at home and in school. She put the family in touch with support groups and visited special schools with the boys' mother when Carlo was in Year 6. Once Carlo had an offer of a place at his special school, Sue liaised with the pastoral care manager and SENCO to ensure that the transition was successful and that he would have the care he required in his new school.

Points for practice

The points to pay attention to in this case study are that the home/school support worker:

- arranged and facilitated meetings between agencies and between parents and agencies
- provided the information to Petros in a manner he could access to enable treatment to take place
- helped Sue, the mother, access additional financial and care support from the statutory authorities
- provided consistent and regular support for a number of years, liasing with other agencies and schools, especially at times of transition.

Summary

This chapter has concentrated on looking at ways in which a home/school support worker can enhance a school's pastoral system, by providing additional time, advice, support and information to parents who have special educational needs themselves and/or have children with special educational needs. This type of work needs to be very sensitively handled and can be extremely time-consuming over a long period. By providing regular help, training, or just 'an ear to listen', parents can be encouraged to remain positively engaged with school, enabling the children to be happy and to continue their education. The support worker cannot be expected to be well-informed about all aspects of special educational needs, but it is the willingness to find information or to seek advice from experts that is important here. Parents will not expect a worker to be an expert in special educational needs, recognizing that it is the professionals within the education system who will provide this input. Finally, experience has shown that parents themselves may be experts in the special needs of their children, particularly where the diagnosis has been in place for some time. Many home/school support workers have learned from parents about support groups, best practice and the latest treatments and equipment. This information can then be shared with others with similar problems.

〰️ Points for reflection

1   How does the role of the home/school support worker differ to that of a school SENCO?

2a Return to the case study on page 50 about Lucy and Boris. Reflect carefully on why you think Sam's input at meetings and within the home is so important.

2b Would you feel confident to be able to sustain this level of care and support over a long period of time?

2c What training and support do you think a home/school support worker would require?

2d Are there confidentiality and protection issues here, for both the worker and the family? Discuss.

3a How do you think an issue that involves the special educational needs of a child will differ from one that does not impact on additional programmes or support within school?

3b Reflect on how teachers may feel if they know a home/school support worker is involved in finding a specialist placement for one of their pupils.

3c How can a home/school support worker and a school ensure that they remain functioning well as part of a team when perhaps faced with requests from parents and children which do not coincide with the views of the school?

📖 Further reading

DfES (2001) *Special Educational Needs Code of Practice.* Annesley: DfES. Also at www.teachernet.gov.uk/teachinginengland/detail.cfm?id=390

Soan, S. (ed.) (2005) *Additional Educational Needs.* London: David Fulton.

Useful websites

Citizens Advice Bureau – www.adviceguide.org/nm/index/family_parent/education/special_educational_needs.htm

Department for Schools, Children and Families (DSCF) – www.adviceguide.org/nm/index/family_parent/education/special_educational_needs.htm

Teachernet – www.teachernet.gov.uk/wholeschool/sen

5

Neglect and Poverty

It is important to remember when reading this chapter that 'neglect' and 'poverty' have two very different meanings. 'Poverty' is a term used to define the scarcity of money and food, whereas 'neglect' is used to indicate the failure of a person in giving due care, attention, or time, usually to a child. Therefore, children living in poverty are not necessarily also neglected, and, equally, children who are from affluent, wealthy homes can also be neglected.

In this chapter, the impact of poverty and neglect on children will be discussed together, because they both can lead children to disaffection and despair, frequently causing them to also reject education and school. Poverty in itself, for example, is not indicative of disengagement with education or anti-social behaviours. However, in an affluent society where education is often only nominally free, a child without the correct uniform (whether official or peer-led), without the means to participate in school activities (often due to poor access to transport), and in extreme cases often hungry and tired, is at huge risk of disengaging with his education. Such children may manage to stay out of trouble and improve their prospects, but they are also more likely to suffer both mental and physical ill health.

Neglected children may show signs of distress associated with lack of positive attention and care. They may be attention-seeking and inappropriately clingy to adults; they may, like poor children, present in school as dishevelled and hungry; they may display signs of poor health and growth.

So whether the deprivation suffered by these children is a result of their lack of material means or the paucity of care meted out to them, the effects are detrimental to their well-being, and opportunities to support such children through school should be proactively explored.

Every Child Matters

Be healthy: impact of poverty and neglect on child health
Poor health affects children from low-income families, because of the higher risk that they will not have the opportunity to benefit from a well-balanced,

nutritional diet and appropriate exercise. A lack of exercise and a poor diet can have a lasting impact on their physical and mental outcomes as adults. Where neglect includes the physical well-being of children, the impact on health can also be profound.

Identification

School staff and other family care workers are in contact with children on a regular/daily basis and are uniquely placed to notice signs of neglect and poverty in children. Robust systems of reporting and regularly updated child protection training for the whole staff should ensure that serious instances of neglect are not missed. Signs of neglect and poverty to look out for include children who are regularly:

- dirty
- tired
- hungry
- inadequately or inappropriately dressed for the weather
- chronically ill
- showing a pale or pasty complexion
- smelling unpleasantly
- with untreated ailments or injuries.

In a school setting, children will present with a broad range of health problems due to neglect. These may be as basic as untreated head lice, or as complex as a serious failure to thrive, resulting in poor growth and communication and serious learning and behavioural difficulties, requiring multi-agency intervention. It is important that the less serious problems are dealt with as early as possible, because in this way long-term deeper harm may be prevented from occurring at all.

Intervention

In families where neglect is not serious, but is impacting on a child's ability to concentrate in class, a meeting with parents and an honest expression of concern may be enough to prompt the parent to provide better care. Often, the stress of poverty, financial worries and health concerns that may beset families, leads to the neglect of children, and a conversation with parents about how their actions are impacting on their child, followed by regular contact from a supportive person, makes them aware that their child is valued and cared for in the school environment. It will also gently inform them that neglect is noticed and will be acted upon. Genuine offers of support where neglect is due to poverty issues can be made confidentially through home/school support workers. Intervention may be any of the following:

- **home visiting** as a means to offer support to parents and assure them of the care and concerns of the school
- **reminders and liaison** for health checks and meetings that may involve accompanying parents or helping them to access transport
- **monitoring** of a child's health and development in school through the school nurse service
- **raising awareness** among staff

- **whole school community** policies giving parents information about health issues
- providing children with **confidential support and reassurance**.

It is necessary to keep detailed, *dated* notes on a child who is giving cause for concern in order to keep track of their presentation in school (see Appendix 3). Patterns may emerge through this that will help clarify the extent of the problem. These will represent part of the child's confidential record and must therefore be kept in a secure cabinet. Data may also be asked to be seen at any time and therefore the accuracy of anything recorded is vital. Where necessary, these may form the basis of a referral to another agency.

More severe levels of deprivation with children suffering chronic neglect will require more robust intervention. The school nurse service, health visitors (where pre-school children are involved), social services and the paediatric service may need to be consulted and child protection procedures followed (see case study below).

 Case study: Martha

Martha has four children between the ages of two and seven. She has been abandoned by her most recent partner and suffers from depression. She spends many hours of the day and night on the internet accessing chat rooms. The children have only basic care. Liam, the eldest, has chronic asthma and eczema which is not well managed. He has been sent into school quite poorly with chest infections and high temperatures. He and his sister Sarah often do not have adequate uniform or coats for bad weather. He says that he has to dress himself and a neighbour brings them down to school. There are other health issues around the two younger children who are pre-school.

After a referral from the class teacher who had spoken with Martha on several occasions to no effect, the home/school support worker phoned Martha and made arrangements to visit. She worked with Martha over several months, gaining her trust and encouraging her to take Liam to his appointments. Martha would be very positive one week, keeping the house clean and feeling able to go out, but by the following week she would be depressed and unable to manage even the basic housework.

Interventions involved taking Martha to appointments, liaising with the health visitor team, a referral for Liam to see the school nurse regularly and eventually encouraging Martha to seek help for her depression.

Points for practice

Hence, in this situation outside agencies as well as the school's home/school support worker were involved in ensuring the children were well cared for while still enabling the family to stay together. It was the ability of the school's worker to visit on a regular basis, providing that long-term support that was so vital in this case. Appropriate support could then be given, as the family members were able to accept and recognize that they needed help.

Staying safe: neglect, poverty and risks to safety

Children who are neglected or poor may well face greater risks to personal safety than their peers. If they are unsupervised and undirected, then they are more likely to suffer accidents; they could face potential threats from adults and other children, and there may be more opportunities for them to succumb to peer pressure to drink, smoke or take drugs. Huge differences can exist between children who are deprived and those in the same classroom that are well cared for. This difference is not always apparent to the children themselves when they are small, but past the age of eight they become increasingly aware of their poverty or the gulf of care between them and their peers. Where there is parental neglect, their desire to fit in and belong may make them vulnerable to peer groups and more likely to engage in criminal or risky behaviour. Government initiatives to force parents to take charge where children are out of control take little account of the poor family structures that may have led to the problem(s) in the first place.

Identification

While poverty may make a child dissatisfied with her lot and embarrassed in front of peers, if parental care is good or adequate, then risk of danger or criminality is greatly reduced. Neglected children, however, are far more likely to come to harm through lack of adult direction and supervision and the resulting poor self-esteem. Signs of neglect that might lead to harm include:

- inappropriate risk-taking
- frequent minor untreated injuries
- criminal activities, trespassing, climbing buildings, stealing, fire-setting
- smoking, drinking or drug-taking
- self-harming behaviours, cutting, etc.
- anger, fighting with peers.

Peer problems can start with these children once they are old enough to appreciate what they lack and as peer groups develop and 'fitting in' becomes ever harder. Bullying and isolation may result, adding to the misery. Crucial stages of development, such as the transition to secondary school, can exacerbate the problem, because of the need for specialist equipment and the correct school uniform and PE kit. Depending on the character of the child and what resilience factors they possess, such additional stresses may lead to behaviours that put her at risk.

Interventions

While infant children tend to be more at risk of accidental harm because they are unsupervised, older children are more likely to offend, self-harm, suffer serious accidents and become exposed to drugs or sexual activity. The older the child, the harder it is to intervene successfully; early preventive intervention is very much to be desired. School again is uniquely placed to offer support to children identified as suffering from neglect or poverty; such support can prove invaluable in preventing disaffection. Schools and other agencies can help by the following means:

- School/agency structures are in place to provide clothing and equipment for families who need extra support.
- Identification and tracking systems are in place through schools, enabling children at risk to be monitored closely and therefore quickly supported if a need arises.
- Close engagement with parents to encourage greater involvement in education and the daily lives of their children.
- Confidential support available in school to provide parenting advice or to signpost to local agencies offering necessary and appropriate advice.
- Liaison with police and other agencies to support children at risk of offending.
- Systems in place to enable identified children to access clubs and extended school provision easily and without additional cost.

It must be recognized that parents of neglected children by definition are hard to engage with and, in this, dedicated home/school support workers are uniquely placed to open channels of communication and encourage parental support. By its nature, this may be slow work and improvements may be small; workers should not be discouraged by this. Changes in some families may take generations, and the advantage of the home/school support role is that it does not require instant results and is limited in time only by the child's passage through school.

 Case study: Chris, aged 6

Chris is very small for his age and is often grubby and hungry. He is brought to school by his older sister (eight years) and they are often very early, waiting outside the school gates. Over the course of six months, Chris suffered three serious injuries. He badly gashed his leg, broke his wrist and suffered a concussion. Each time, the injuries occurred while playing out in the street in the evening unsupervised and in dangerous places. Older children raised the alarm and brought Chris home and his mother took him to casualty. In school, Chris continued to be dirty and appointments with the hospital were sometimes missed so Chris's dressings were not always changed.

Following these injuries, the home/school support worker visited Chris's mother and found a chaotic household where Chris was the youngest and was usually left in the care of his older sister, while teenage siblings failed to check up on his whereabouts and welfare.

She suggested to Chris's mother that Chris and his sister should attend the breakfast club in school as she left early for work. She would then know that the children were safe in the mornings. She was offered help to pay for this through the school welfare fund for part of the week. There were several evening clubs and she engaged Chris and his sister in these also.

During the holidays, she accessed several play schemes, some with free places for Chris and his sister to attend; transport was a problem, but another local family whose children were friendly with Chris offered to help here.

She then began regularly engaging with Chris's mother to offer support and to keep in touch. In school, the community police officer came to speak to all the children about playing safely.

Points for practice

Assumptions were not quickly made about the family in this situation and notes were kept over a long period of time. However, the family worker carefully monitored the children's health and safety and, when action was needed, went to speak to the mother in the first instance. Positive support was possible in this case because the school and the local community had established clubs and groups which could help keep children safe and well cared for. The only agency involved at this stage was introduced through a group initiative, meaning that the child was not made to feel that he had been 'wrong' or 'bad', but was nevertheless given the information he required to enable him to think about his risk-taking behaviour. It is important to remember that appropriate intervention and support does not have to involve outside agencies and extreme forms of action.

 ## Case study: Elijah, aged 16

Elijah attends a large high school and has struggled with poverty for the last five years. He is currently taking his GCSE exams and is living in a bed-sit with his mother and young brother. She is a refugee whose husband has deserted her and has no family locally. Elijah had an accident on his bike several days ago and has a large open wound on his hip where he fell. His mother has bought dressings but there are not enough and she is afraid the wound is not healing.

In school, Elijah presents as a loner; he is very thin and pale looking and has a limited wardrobe of well-worn clothes. Elijah was identified as needy three years ago by his home/school support worker, Mike. He has put Elijah's mother in touch with refugee support agencies and charities who have helped her out at various times. She is currently on a housing list and the home/school worker is in regular touch with the local housing officer. Elijah knows to come to Mike when things are not going well and trusts him, though he does tend to leave it until things are really bad. Mike makes regular checks to see how Elijah is coping and picked up that he was uncomfortable and in pain. He organized for Elijah to go to the local treatment clinic to have his dressing changed before his exams and has found him new clothes and trainers. He has also checked with Elijah that he has the correct equipment for the exams he must sit. Elijah's mother regularly comes to see Mike and tells him how she is getting on. Mike has promised to support Elijah if he chooses to stay in school for sixth form.

Points for practice

In this case study, the need for staff to be constantly on hand to notice changes in children and young people can be clearly identified.

The important elements the worker in this situation was involved in included:

- monitoring housing arrangements
- physical care
- illustrating the value of education
- a close working relationship with the young person's mother
- a good knowledge of how the young person acted
- the understanding that additional practical, as well as emotional support, i.e. equipment for examinations, may well be required.

This case study also illustrates the importance of seeing the child/young person in a holistic way, which included, in this instance, the need to support his mother and also to monitor housing and health issues. The development of an appropriate and trusting relationship with the young person and their family/carers was vital in this situation. Without this, Elijah's wound may well have been left to fester, and his ability to cope with school life far less likely.

Enjoy and achieve: educational effects of neglect and poverty

There are well-established studies to show that children who are well supported by their parents throughout their education achieve more academically and are more successful as adults (Desforges and Abouchaar, 2003). On the other hand, children whose parents either won't or can't engage with schools do less well and, in extreme cases, fail to stay in school, refusing or being excluded. Conclusions from such research indicate that both neglect and poverty seem to adversely affect children's ability to engage with learning.

Identification

Some children are emotionally neglected by parents who show little real interest in their well-being and achievements, even though there are no signs of physical neglect. Such children are harder to spot and may appear clingy, attention-seeking and show little educational progress. Children who are living in some kind of poverty disengage with education because basic needs may not be being met. They may be tired, cold, hungry, worried and anxious and in such a state that learning is much harder. The effects of poverty and neglect on emotional and educational well-being include:

- chronic anxiety, sadness, depression, forgetfulness
- poor concentration
- poor progress, lack of any progress or regression
- attention-seeking and distracting behaviours
- withdrawal and failure to engage
- lack of parental interest in parents' evenings, school performances, outings and trips, etc.

- lack of school equipment, homework, project material, etc.
- little or no financial support, trip money, charity money.

As many of these symptoms may be associated with other causes, such as bereavement, family crises, divorce and separation, the identification of children who are neglected or poor would require knowledge of other factors, such as their physical well-being and family circumstances. Again, the older the child, the harder it is to discover what is really wrong and to engage with families to find a way forward. Often, a family situation only comes to light with some serious crisis and children are left suffering and coping for many years. These years of struggle add up to considerable damage and loss of opportunity which again highlights the importance of early identification and intervention.

Interventions

It is worth considering here the different approaches possible with Key Stages 1 and 2 and Key Stages 3 and 4. Geographically, most children will live near to their primary school and parents visit more frequently, having more regular contact with staff and other families. Secondary schools have difficulty engaging with parents and finding out about home circumstances. If children are identified as at risk of failing while attending primary school and information can be forwarded during transition to secondary school, outcomes for the children may improve with continuity of support. Transition and transfer between schools could potentially lead to confusion and loss of what support has been put in place and this should be avoided at all cost.

Key Stages 1 and 2

Class teachers are generally the first to notice the poor progress a child is making and to contact parents to notify them and investigate reasons. Simple interventions like regular reporting in a home/school contact book or a prearranged regular phone call to update parents on the child's progress can be tried. Where parents are still reluctant to engage, then careful noting and monitoring of the child's presentation and progress with a referral to the home/school support worker and senior management team may well be thought necessary. Poor progress may well also involve the SENCO or Inclusion Manager, and an in-school meeting with the parents should be arranged involving at least two members of staff to talk about the needs of the child.

If parents are not prepared to come to school, then a different venue or means of discussion needs to be actively sought.

Further interventions might include:

- regular meetings with the family with staff members who support the child
- home visits to assess what help might be needed (again, following school policies on health and safety grounds)
- where families are reluctant to engage, regular reminders of the nature of the concern for the child. Do not give up; parents will often begin to effect changes because school continues to exert pressure. A balance has to be achieved between angering and alienating a family and reminding them of their obligation to their child's education

- offers of help to engage children with extended school activities
- invitations to the wider family to become interested in the child and support the child. Absent fathers, aunts and uncles and grandparents, and even older siblings can show an interest which may make a huge difference
- financial assistance offered in confidence to those families unable to provide for their children's educational needs.

Remember however that your safety is of paramount importance and school/agency health and safety policies should be followed at all times. Taking *risks* with your own safety will not help anyone.

Key Stages 3 and 4
The most important intervention at this stage is the liaison between schools when a child transfers. Not only is support much harder to provide at secondary school, but travel difficulties, peer pressure and increased demands for homework and out-of-school study will increase the chances of an unsupported child failing. Many neglected and poor children begin secondary school without the proper equipment or uniform at a time when most children are being provided with several hundred pounds worth of clothing and accessories. Failing at this stage could be about not having a pair of the 'right' shoes. Schools can be insensitive to these issues and will give a child a detention for wearing the wrong clothing when it is beyond the family's means to provide it. One boy took to truanting because his only footwear was a pair of oversized red trainers which were both against school rules and ridiculous to his peer group. Faced with these options, many such children will either fail to attend or misbehave. Interventions at this stage should therefore bear in mind the mental well-being of the children concerned and their sensibilities. They have to fit in with their peers if they are to engage with school.
  Examples of intervention include:

- a good welfare network within school to identify and approach at-risk children with realistic and confidential offers of help
- some regular and robust attempt at parental contact that reminds parents of their duty or offers help where there is financial need
- good networking with local and national agencies and charities that can provide support for such children
- drop-ins and time out for children having difficulty coping
- a whole school ethos that does not penalize or alienate children whose circumstances do not enable them to afford the right uniform or equipment.

Making a positive contribution: social exclusion
By definition, social exclusion follows from lack of care and poverty in a society that demands financial means to take part and children require adult support to join in with their peers. At primary level, children whose homes are 'no go' areas due to adult indifference or poor housing are not able to have friends

round to tea. They will not be invited back and they will gradually learn not to ask. Close-knit social groups where families are related or have been settled in an area for many generations may support children that have little care or means.

Difficulties are more profound for families who have moved into an area either as migrants or as a result of family crises, etc. If they face social isolation due to language barriers, limited access to benefits, housing difficulties, as well as poverty, then their difficulties are extreme. Victims of domestic violence or those forced to move because of debt are similarly isolated. School may provide families who don't fit in with their best chance of social integration and support. It is the first place they will go to register children on arrival and the most consistent place they will be in contact with for many years.

Identification

Some obvious areas of concern will be:

- children who never attend extracurricular activities
- children who are friendless
- children who have moved school frequently
- children whose parents do not attend meetings or events
- hard-to-contact families where mobile phone numbers are changed and school is not notified
- children who are bullied.

While neglect and poverty set a child apart, there will be those who target them, name-call and bully them, leading to further isolation and disaffection.

Interventions

Integrating children whose circumstances conspire to isolate them becomes harder with age. However, strengthening a supportive peer group and encouraging friendships can offset these difficulties, particularly during transitions between schools. Interventions of this nature could include:

- in-school responsibilities and inclusion in groups – youth councils, peer mentoring, lunch clubs, etc.
- encouraging and enabling parents to attend local support and community groups
- accessible hardship funds to provide the means to attend trips, school journeys, etc.
- peer support and anti-bullying strategies as part of the school ethos.

In ideal circumstances, a significant adult should be identified who can take a special interest in a child and support her through her education. This proves difficult for many reasons, depending on the circumstances of the family, but is always a good target to aim for.

Case study: Nula, aged 7, and Simon, aged 5

Nula and Simon attend their local primary school which is five minutes' walk from their house. They walk themselves in every day and enjoy school. Both their parents work and staff are aware that their care and hygiene is not good. Nula has thick, dark hair and usually has head lice; Simon is shaved close but also has lice. Their parents are very hard to contact and react angrily if they are called at work. Nula is just beginning to notice that she is different, less well cared for than her peers and is not able to have friends round to play. Her home/school worker has been able to sort out her head lice after several phone calls home. Nula's head was extremely sore and with the eventual permission of her parents the school nurse and a teaching assistant began treating the lice on the understanding that Nula's mother would do the same at home. This was successful but the lice did return. During this intervention, a young woman came to the school to pick up Nula and Simon and introduced herself as their aunt. She offered to help with the head lice treatment. The home/school support worker notified Nula's mother who did not object.

With the support of her teacher, Nula was elected a school councillor and thoroughly enjoyed this. Nula's aunt began playing a more active role in the children's lives with the support of the home/school worker and even attended a parents' evening. The home/school support worker arranged for her to be given copies of school newsletters and other information.

Nula and Simon will continue to need extra help and support.

Points for practice

This case study again demonstrates very clearly how a great deal of support can be given to families, enabling trust and a positive relationship to be built. Recognizing the needs of the children, the school – the teachers and teaching assistants, as well as the family worker – went about solving the health and social exclusion issue (head lice) and then tried to support the inclusion of Nula into a role which would be seen as a positive one by her peers. Working with the aunt enabled positive feedback, as well as physical support and action from a family member, providing a good role model for the children. As is said, monitoring and support are likely to be required long term, but by acting on the lower-level needs of the children, hopefully any greater level of care will be quickly identified. In such a case, dated, well-kept notes of action taken, support given and progress made need to be kept by the school.

Achieving economic well-being

Home/school liaison workers have often been initially placed in schools where there is an identified need within a community that in some way acts to prevent full educational achievement. One such need is poverty and workers will often find themselves operating within communities where poverty is widespread and more severe than averages for the United Kingdom in general. Poor communities may also contain ethnic minorities who have entered the country as asylum seekers, communities suffering the effects of job closures, deprivation due to shortages of affordable or adequate housing, and groups with long-term employment and disaffection issues. Poverty is still very much a trap with added costs for those on low incomes that others do not need to incur. Examples include: one client who was charged £50 by her bank every time she went overdrawn even by a few pounds, while the bank refused her overdraft facilities because of her poor debt record; a major loan firm operating within a community on a door-to-door basis lending small sums of a few hundred pounds and charging 40 per cent interest; a client escaping domestic violence who was refused legal aid because she had managed to sustain a part-time job and was earning £30 a month too much.

Complications and restrictions on benefits and tax credits, penalties for non-disclosure of information and difficulties with transport to offices may further erode efforts of self-help. The effects of poverty on generations of children raised in these circumstances include a wide range of educational and social disadvantages.

Identification
Signs in school include:

- poor presentation
- non-payment of dinner money and other fees
- children who never have pocket money or resources
- children lacking shoes or in very cheap shoes
- non-participation in school trips, sponsored events, etc.

We have mentioned shoes as one of the most obvious indicators as good children's shoes are one of the most expensive items a parent will have to regularly buy. Good shoe shops are often located in larger towns requiring transport and many poorer parents make do with shoes bought from cheap outlets. These are replaced infrequently and children will often come into school with shoes that are falling apart or inappropriate. Children from poorer families in primary schools, for example, may well wear cheap fashion boots, ill-fitting shoes, cheap trainers, and light shoes in bad weather.

Interventions
For this, good contacts with housing and benefits agencies are necessary. Access to local charities and projects can provide useful information and funds. Housing and poverty concerns can be acute and tackling this is very difficult. Once the family has accepted help and acknowledged the problem, then some steps forward can be made. Keeping the children engaged with education is hugely important as their future welfare will depend on this.

To achieve this, try to:

- offer realistic support through good local networks
- enable families to claim whatever benefits they are entitled to

- provide signposting to help parents to access job and educational information
- keep the children engaged with school through provision of resources.

It is distressing and worrying to acknowledge that chronic poverty is still a major problem for many children and that adequate help to alleviate this is hard to come by. The case study below shows you how a family worker supported a family in such a situation.

 Case study: Louise

Louise has recently separated from a violent and abusive partner. He has left her with several thousand pounds worth of debts in her name, mostly to loan companies. She has four children and is living in an unfurnished flat found for her by a refuge. She has no furniture and the flat needs some major repairs. Her alternative was bed and breakfast through the local council and the refuge could not accommodate her 15-year-old son. All the children are regularly attending school where they receive free school meals. Their school dinner is their most nutritious meal. Louise has managed after several weeks to organize her benefits and tax credits. She now has her rent and council tax paid, but has agreements to pay arrears of several hundred pounds on both. She is also paying off an emergency loan to the benefits agency. In school, the younger children appear tired and cling to each other. They have incomplete school uniform with trainers instead of the required school shoes. The primary school home/school worker was notified by the children's teachers and Louise was willing to accept any help offered by her. Over the next few weeks this help included:

- dealing first with immediate need through Social Services and local charities to find funds for furniture, bedding, etc., and then ensuring there was food and clothing, heating, lighting and cooking facilities for the children and Louise
- contacting the local housing department to ensure that Louise was placed on the housing list
- enabling Louise to access financial help to reduce her debts
- supporting the children in school with school and local charitable funds to provide equipment, uniform and shoes
- liaising with Louise to ensure the children have access to medical and dental services.

Points for practice

Accepting help can be very difficult, but Louise recognized the needs of her children and the benefits of schooling. Louise knew that the younger children would receive a wholesome meal once a day at school and was able to accept help to provide her children with the equipment, uniform and shoes they required. Tact and understanding are vital in such a situation. The worker in this instance was working with a mother who wanted to care for her children, but needed help to do so. Again, trust and careful, considerate discussion can enable the children to gain the physical as well as the social and emotional support they would need to be able to access and engage with learning. Longer-term emotional issues for the children may well still occur, but it is hoped that if and when this happens, the mother (Louise) will be able to work positively with family and school workers to help the children overcome these as well. By then, a trusting and respectful relationship will have been developed.

Multi-agency working

Poverty and neglect involve child protection issues that include emotional harm, exposure to danger and physical failure to thrive. Interagency working will need to involve agencies that have statutory duties, i.e. Social Services, health and educational services, police, housing and benefits agencies. Engaging with these services should now be an automatic part of working within children's services, and setting up and maintaining good contacts with these agencies should be part of a school's working practice.

Preventive strategies to enable children who are at risk of educational disaffection due to poverty or neglect should involve strong teams. Children registered on Social Services' Tiers 3 and 4 (Child Protection Registered and Looked After Children) will still be regularly attending school and home/school liaison staff should be represented at meetings for these children. Children requiring lower-tier intervention, who are giving cause for concern, are better helped with strong interagency teams served by regular information exchanges. Families should be informed of the agencies concerned and proper referrals made where necessary.

Non-statutory agencies and charities can be very useful in supporting families in these circumstances, especially where they are very local and experienced in dealing with local concerns. Community centres, Citizen's Advice Bureaux, churches and other faith centres, welfare associations and charities may all be able to help out with particular needs. Local areas often have charities supplying good second-hand furniture and other goods, and are often better at donating small sums of money quickly in order to alleviate immediate need.

Some home/school support workers hold regular meetings in local areas to meet with statutory and non-statutory agencies and charities and establish good links. Some useful organizations to identify and try to build contacts with include:

- the Citizen's Advice Bureau who can offer free debt counselling and management
- St Vincent de Paul Society, Round Table, Lions Club and other local charities who can offer financial assistance and visiting
- youth and community groups who may be able to offer mentoring and support for young people

- family centres and community groups aimed at supporting particular minority groups who can offer advice, support at meetings, translating, etc.
- community police and youth-offending prevention teams.

Your local area will have its own network of support and advice and this should be accessed and links established.

General points for practice

Confidentiality and child protection

For practical and management reasons, Child Protection Officers should *not* be home/school support workers, because there will be a conflict of interest between these two roles.

Child protection issues within schools should be monitored with a robust system that identifies and keeps a record of concerns over time. Families that are giving cause for concern should be regularly reviewed to ensure that signs are not missed and that the school is doing all it can to support the children (see Appendices 1, 2 and 5).

Where multi-agency consultation occurs, families should be informed where child safety is not compromised. Open and transparent working with families helps to strengthen trust. Agencies working separately for the same family should liaise and let the family know they are doing so. In this way, lapses in care can be avoided. Some agencies are better at this than others and home/school support workers tend to have good relationships with the school nurse service, health visitors and community police. For many practical reasons, agencies that cover wide areas such as hospitals, Social Services, housing departments, etc. can be harder to engage with. Where other agencies are being brought in, clear referrals with parental consent should be made where possible.

The emphasis should be to work alongside parents to encourage their use of services.

Schools working together

Where home/school support exists in several schools within an area, regular meetings between workers in these schools can be a very effective way of networking, supporting local families and providing help for children during transition to secondary school. Such meetings can host local service providers, education officers and voluntary agencies to discuss joint working and ideas (see Appendix 6). Accessing funding for alleviating poverty, for training courses and advice for parents trying to move forward, and establishing local support networks can all be facilitated through these meetings. Individual families should *never* be discussed at these meetings and confidentiality should be borne in mind at all times.

Close working between schools will help to maintain support for families struggling with poverty and children experiencing neglect. Many such families move schools regularly, never settling in one place, especially where poor housing is an issue. If schools are communicating regularly, then children are less likely to slip through the net.

Moving a child with these problems successfully on to secondary school will require good communication between primary and secondary schools.

Contacting parents

Once concerns have been raised about a child, maybe by a teacher, learning mentor or teaching assistant, then the parents or carers of that child should be approached and notified. There are some simple rules for these approaches that enable a home/school support worker or teaching member of staff to begin to build a relationship with a parent/carer:

1 **Confidentiality:** initial approaches should allow the parent/carer privacy in discussing what may be sensitive issues. If the parent is met at the school gate, then asking them to step inside to a more private space before beginning to explain concerns does two things: it tells them that your concerns are of a serious nature and that you respect their right to privacy. It also gives them an opportunity if they so desire to open up and tell you more.
2 **Patience:** where issues are chronic and the family has been used to dealing with them for many years, they will not be solved overnight and the family will not open up immediately. Maintaining contact and waiting patiently for responses tells the parent/carer that you will be continuing to monitor the situation and that you are there to offer help when they are ready. This is often enough to change circumstances, particularly when the child has been neglected. The parent's knowing that this has been noticed may encourage them to give more care.
3 **Be ready to listen:** it is not necessary or possible to solve every problem that a family presents you with; listening may be a first step in a long journey that the parent/carer must travel to effect change.
4 **Clarity:** making clear what help is available and how to access it; stating how and when a parent can come for help and giving choices where appropriate.
5 **Signposting:** where appropriate, referring and signposting parents/carers to other agencies, both statutory and non-statutory.
6 **Consultation:** keeping parents informed of all interventions and seeking their permission to consult with other agencies/schools, etc.

Summary

This chapter has illustrated the importance of schools developing robust strategies to monitor and address neglect and poverty in individual pupils. It has highlighted the need for good recording, confidential and sensitive communication with parents, interagency referral where necessary and multi-agency working. The importance of schools in recognizing signs of proverty and neglect has been emphasised. We have also provided examples of how schools might alleviate the effects of poor care on educational outcomes. Finally it has shown the importance of good local knowledge of community needs and resources.

〰️Points for reflection

The following questions should help an institution such as a school, or an individual worker, consider the many issues discussed in this chapter. Every situation and need is different, but with:

- a sound ethos (school's/agency's)
- good recording and monitoring systems
- a holistic approach to meeting children's needs
- good networking and multi-agency working systems
- time and trust built through developing relationships

children can be positively supported in remaining engaged in education and learning.

1 How good is your school or agency at establishing and building local networks and links in an attempt to foster support networks for families in poverty, or children experiencing neglect? Think carefully about:

- who is in charge of developing community and charity links
- what systems/information your school or agency has in place to help support families financially, medically, practically (e.g. housing) and to track the impact on children and young people (shoes, equipment, clothing, etc.)
- how you respond to issues of neglect?

2 Are staff actively encouraged to identify and monitor the holistic needs of the children they work with? For example, does a teacher or teaching assistant know who to go to if a child has poor clothing, extremely bad head lice or health issues, and is there a monitored way of tracking these concerns?

3 How good are your systems at monitoring and tracking the progress of children with regard to their social inclusion and physical well-being, as well as to their educational progress? How frequently is this monitored? Who is responsible for ensuring this takes place and how is it tracked?

4 What health and safety policies are in place to ensure staff are protected from physical or emotional harm when working with families requiring a great deal of support? Are these well known and regularly updated? Is advice gained from the local community police or social services?

5 Is the time required to carry out such work appropriate and is it considered a long-term issue? How does such work fit into your local extended school's projects and development plans?

📖 Further reading

DfES (2006) *Safeguarding Children and Safer Recruitment in Education*. Annesley: DfES.

Wilkin, A., Kinder, K., White, R., Atkinson, M. and Doherty, P. (2003) *Towards the Development of Extended Schools*. NFER Research Report 408. Annesley: DfES.

Useful websites

Child Protection – www.everychildmatters.gov.uk/socialcare/safeguarding

Citizen Advice Bureau – www.citizensadvice.org.uk

Lions Club – www.lions.org.uk

Round Table – www.roundtable.co.uk

St Vincent de Paul Society – www.svp.org.uk

Teachernet – www.teachernet.gov.uk/wholeschool/familyandcommunity/childprotection

Youth Groups – www.need2know.co.uk/time_out/get_involved

6

Anger and Social, Emotional and Behavioural Needs

In this chapter, home/school support workers, learning mentors and specialist teaching assistants will be helped to consider and explore ways of:

- supporting a family with a disturbed and badly behaved child, thus helping to support positive behaviour and learning in school
- helping children control their anger or behaviour through school and home-based interventions.

Children who exhibit social, emotional and behavioural difficulties (SEBD) may have a number of reasons for their behaviour. These may include:

- manifesting outward signs of a learning difficulty that is affecting their ability to cope with the social and educational pressures
- being poorly parented
- suffering crises and disruption in the home
- being emotionally disturbed by a traumatic event.

This chapter will consider ways in which specialist staff members might help prevent the exclusion or disaffection of such children through help in school and at home, or by support from other agencies. Other agencies in this situation include Child and Adolescent Mental Health Services (CAMHS), Specialist Teaching Services and Primary Intervention Projects. Even when such services are in place and advice is given to schools, the reality of day-to-day handling is often very difficult and may involve considerable stress for staff members. We will consider how schools as a whole, and individual staff members, working together with parents/carers can make considerable improvements to the ways in which such children are helped and responded to.

Every Child Matters

One teacher who had spent his whole career in specialist provision for children with behavioural difficulties stated that such children were 'socially handicapped' and that they often failed to excite the sympathy of others because they were seen as in some way to blame for their behaviour. Certainly, it is true that other parents will tolerate a child with learning difficulties or a physical disability in a classroom, but will feel that there is a considerable threat to their child in the presence of a child with behavioural problems. Whatever the cause of such problems, they will impact hugely on that child's ability to fulfil their educational potential and may also adversely affect the learning of their peers.

Practice in schools now may involve a child being given access to a learning mentor, a specialist teaching assistant or a home/school support worker who will implement strategies designed to help the child overcome the barriers to learning that their behaviour represents.

Teaching practice with its current emphasis on targets and examinations will pose a threat to children who find classroom discipline, concentration and social interaction difficult. Learning styles in these children may favour a more hands-on practical approach and this is often unavailable consistently in mainstream schools. Managing behavioural difficulties to help these children achieve their full potential requires an approach that does not try to change the child to fit the school, but rather considers more flexible ways to enable that child to cope better.

Being healthy: emotional well-being and behavioural difficulties
Identification

Many children with social, emotional and behavioural difficulties will present as deeply unhappy with very low self-esteem. They will describe themselves as 'mad' or 'crazy', 'bad boy/girl', 'hateful', and will often feel stupid and a failure in the classroom. These feelings in an adult could easily be described as a form of depression, and in children may actually have the same effect. Social and emotional difficulties will also include any failure to interact, whether or not that child is disruptive or angry, so would encompass the following:

- withdrawal
- sullenness
- refusal to comply
- running away and refusing to attend
- social isolation among peers
- inappropriate attention-seeking
- hugging and clinging to adults.

Such children may also bully or be bullied, or perceive themselves to be bullied. All these thoughts and feelings contribute to poor mental-health outcomes. Some factors indicating this include:

- low self-esteem, speaking of themselves as worthless or stupid
- poor educational progress and failure to engage in learning
- running away, out of class or out of the school building, and school refusing
- excessive and age-inappropriate behaviours, sulking, temper tantrums, etc.
- sadness
- extreme behaviours–self-harming and talking of suicide, hurting others, risk-taking, drug abuse.

Once identified, the underlying problems should be explored by the school team responsible. This team is likely to include the class teacher, SENCO, head teacher, home/school support worker and specialist teaching assistant. With outside agency help, where necessary, a clear plan of approach should be drawn up, including parent contact and support.

Interventions

Outcomes for children are always better when supported by a team of people and when the intervention is known to all the adults who have contact with that child. It is no good drawing up a plan for an angry child that includes a 'time out' card if a staff member does not know to recognize it and grant the child his space. Similarly, supply teachers and temporary staff members should be given relevant information about the programme for a child.

Close working with the parents reassures them that school is working towards a solution and cares about the child's educational future, and offers valuable support to parents who may feel isolated and desperate in the face of extreme behaviour.

Interventions that focus on the health and well-being of the child may include:

- regular opportunities to talk about feelings and express anger appropriately
- firm boundaries and clear staff directions to deal with outbursts of violence; where appropriate, positive handling and restraint training
- time out and places of safety, and named adults who can be called to deal with a child
- appropriate support for staff involved
- good home/school contact that can update staff if there are changes at home that might impact on the child's health and well-being
- an awareness of the impact on behaviour that illness and poor health can have.

The last suggestion should be borne in mind particularly where a child's behaviour suddenly changes for the worse. The first thing to investigate is whether that child is sick or in pain, as children can sometimes be unable to express their hurt or discomfort in any other way. If an adult goes into work with a severe headache, then no one would be too surprised to find them bad tempered or snappy.

Case study: Oliver, aged 8

Oliver's mother Coral moved away from a difficult relationship taking Oliver and his younger sister, aged 4, back to her parents. Her father has Alzheimer's and her mother struggles to cope with him. Coral now shares a small flat with her parents and is on the local authority housing list. Oliver is diagnosed with ADHD and sleeps very little. His grandfather is often awake in the night and disturbs the children further. Coral has a brother who is violent and controlling and often comes round and threatens her. Oliver has twice been found harming himself, once with a plastic bag over his head and a second time deeply scratching his arms with a nail. He talks about wanting to die to his mother. In his previous school, he was seeing a mental health worker, but there is a long waiting list in his new area. In school, he is disruptive and runs away. He has also lashed out and hurt other children.

There is a home/school support worker in his current school and a specialist teaching assistant has been assigned to him to help him cope with his learning environment. The SENCO has contacted the CAMHS team in his previous area and has asked them for information about the help he needs; she has also made an emergency referral to the local CAMHS team because of Oliver's self-harming behaviour. His previous school has also been contacted. Safe adults have been identified that Oliver trusts and can ask for if he feels threatened or anxious. He has behaviour charts and works in supervised small groups. Playtimes are supervised by his TA. The home/school support worker has been helping Coral with housing, benefits and her relationships with her family. This has included a self-referral to Social Services, counselling and liaison with the local police domestic violence unit to help her deal with her brother. Visiting the flat raises safety issues for the home/school support worker because of the threat from Coral's brother. They either meet in school or at a local café.

Points for practice

In this case study, the home/school support worker is part of a team working together to try to support this family and, in particular, Oliver. The school helped Oliver with his learning and behaviour needs in school. However, the home/school worker was able to help Oliver's mother practically, which in turn will impact positively on Oliver. It is important yet again to remember that the worker 'helps' Coral gain help and ask for assistance, but does not actually 'do' anything for her. The role needs to respect and demand that the worker helps the family make the changes for themselves, empowering them and giving them greater control over their own lives and futures. It is hoped that in this way the family will sustain their control and will make steady progress.

Staying safe
Identification
Behaviours that mark out a child as being at risk of harm may involve children who have a poor prediction and avoidance of danger, or who appear not to care about their own physical safety. The former can be due to inappropriate parenting, neglect, learning difficulties or immaturity, while the later may be associated with low self-esteem, mental-health issues and depression. The most obvious risk to safety occurs in children who are violent and bully others where there is intent to harm and risk of retaliation, as well as accidental serious harm when an attack gets out of hand and children run, climb, stumble, etc. Children who are violent are also at risk of harm from older children, threats from older siblings, gang violence in older children, possible use of weapons, and violence from adults. Some of these issues have already been discussed in the chapter on domestic violence.

Children who have behaviour problems are also at risk of:

- accident and injury from risk-taking activities
- playing in unsafe places
- experimenting with drugs, alcohol and cigarettes
- approaching adults who are strangers
- making enemies of other children who are violent.

There are several lines of referral for these children depending on the nature of their behavioural difficulties. Within school, the home/school intervention should begin as soon as possible, as good parental involvement could greatly increase the chance of successful outcomes. All too often, intervention does not start until there is a risk of exclusion and parents are reluctant to engage, feeling threatened, responsible and guilty about their child's problem. Good referrals pinpoint children:

- who show aggression towards other pupils and/or adults
- whose parents have reported behavioural difficulties at home and have asked for help
- where local reports have identified them as causing violence within the community
- where local reports have identified them as playing dangerously
- where there is evidence of substance abuse or criminal behaviour.

None of these signs should be ignored, even if they are minor or first-time occurrences; some consequences should always be demonstrated.

Interventions
Involvement of parents/carers should happen at the earliest opportunity and the school could make it clear that they aim to offer constructive support to the family. A dedicated home/school support worker can encourage the parent's engagement with school and any other agencies, while ensuring that the difficulties are not ignored by the family and encouraging them to take an active

part in solving them. Other interventions must aim to minimize the harm done to other children and the threat to staff members including the home/school worker. Interventions to improve behaviour are covered at length in many publications. Here we will give examples of interventions specifically suited to members of staff with pastoral support roles. Interventions include:

- Small group work looking at anger management, self-esteem and social skills where there is identified need.
- Close home/school liaison including parenting courses, small support groups and home visiting where appropriate.
- Whole school involvement in anti-bullying, respect agendas, peer mentoring and restorative justice.
- Close monitoring and analysis of triggers and danger areas; asking where and why a child loses control or misbehaves and implementing policies that prevent this, e.g. lunchtime supervised activities, chaperoning on transport or parent involvement with transportation.
- Clear boundary setting and consequences for infringements in conjunction with parents, so there is continuity between home and school, and parents are encouraged to support school discipline.
- Relevant referrals to other agencies that can support and help.
- Whole staff understanding of the strategies being employed to manage and support a child.

Again, these interventions work best where the workers concerned are a team with regular meetings and appropriate training. All relevant workers should attend in-school and multi-agency meetings concerning a child, so that support workers are given the opportunity to see the whole picture and give their views on ways forward.

 Case study: Eli, aged 11

Eli is moving to secondary school in six month's time. He has mild dyslexia and stammers, is very tall for his age and is concerned about the transfer. Eli has always had a bad temper and has been in trouble in school for this. He has occasional detentions for fighting and disruptive behaviour in class, but is not seen as an unmanageable pupil. His mother came to see the home/school support worker because his behaviour at home had deteriorated. He had been coming home late and was caught smoking. He is mixing with an older peer group that is regularly in trouble and was reported for stealing from the local supermarket. He is also playing a game that involves trespassing in dangerous places: railway lines, substations, building sites and rooftops. His parents are extremely worried about him.

Eli began one-to-one meetings with the home/school support worker to talk about his concerns. She has informed him that she is working closely with

(Continued)

(Continued)

his parents and he has admitted stealing and trespassing. The home/school worker is also liaising with the local police Youth Offending Team and Community Police Officer and Eli has been visited and warned about his behaviour. Through the home/school support worker, Eli has been invited to attend a week of transition events during the school holidays at his new school. His new school has been informed of his difficulties and is putting into place anger management sessions and peer mentoring. The school nurse has spoken to Eli about his smoking.

Concerns still remain about the company Eli keeps and his parents' ability to enforce groundings.

Points for practice

In this case study, there are a number of points that illustrate clearly how an effective home/school worker carries out his role. Firstly, he considers himself part of a team working with other professionals helping a young person make a successful transfer to secondary school. He then helps the young person in a number of practical ways. He:

- gives him opportunities to talk about his needs and his views
- arranges for a school nurse to help him practically with his smoking addiction
- ensures Eli is aware that his parents are extremely concerned about him and his behaviour, and that the school, the worker and his parents are in regular contact
- informs the new school and assists in setting up a programme to support his anger difficulties
- arranges an opportunity for Eli to get to know his new school prior to the start of term.

These actions will not solve Eli's problems, but they highlight for him a number of significant factors. Firstly, the interventions show Eli that his school is concerned about him and his learning and behaviour, and that they are working hard to support his transfer to his new secondary school. He can also see that his parents are extremely worried and are working closely with his school to try and address his anger needs, his smoking habit and his disaffections with learning. These are all points that show him that there are adults who are working together to help him access learning and develop his skills.

Enjoy and achieve: the barriers posed by behaviour difficulties

It is clear that serious levels of disruptive and difficult behaviour severely disrupt children's learning and prevent them from achieving their full potential. In extreme cases, where frequent exclusions take place, then absence from school leads to poor educational outcomes with children falling behind their peers and finding it hard to reintegrate. Furthermore, behavioural problems affect a child's ability to socialize successfully with poor choices of friendships and cycles of misbehaviour leading to alienation and further poor choices. Early intervention with appropriate family support can break these cycles, and close working with school to improve educational outcomes can make a difference between continued disaffection and re-engagement with education.

Identification

There are children whose behaviour is obviously causing low academic outcomes and failure to achieve in school. Their regular punishments and the threats of exclusion fail to effect any change and attempted interventions are met with resistance and non-compliance. There are also children where the reason for failure to achieve is more difficult to identify and where engagement with the education process is minimal. In either of these cases, identification involves the monitoring of both academic achievement and social interaction. Some useful indicators for children with these needs are:

- friendship problems leading to inability to engage in learning and disruption of lessons
- continued poor progress despite interventions to address behavioural problems
- unhappiness and withdrawal
- parent reports of poor behaviour.

Behavioural problems are usually obvious within a school setting. Badly behaved and disturbed children can cause disruption to mainstream lessons and stress to staff and other pupils. For children who have failed to respond to routine interventions and discipline, more creative and multi-disciplinary working needs to be tried. The involvement of parents at every stage strengthens the power of the intervention, particularly if the parents can see some positive outcomes in the home environment.

Intervention

Specific interventions need to be targeted at helping the child to attain and close the gap between them and their peers, particularly where poor behaviour has led to exclusions and disaffection. The cycle of failure to learn due to behavioural difficulties, followed by a widening gap between a child and their peers, leading to further isolation, needs to be recognized and addressed. While discipline and punishment can involve extra work, catch-up and completion of missed homework, etc., this does not really serve to encourage the child to enjoy and achieve in their education. More positive and encouraging lines of work may include:

- A creative curriculum tailored to the learning style of the pupil.
- A consideration of the talents of the pupil and encouraging parents to provide extracurricular lessons or activities around these.
- Engaging the parent in the education of their child through helping out in school, attending school trips and activities, etc.
- Working with the child to identify their own worries and concerns and giving the child opportunities to express their views. Do they understand the impact of their behaviour on learning and do they wish to improve?

- Using learning mentors, peer mentors, specialist teaching assistants, etc. to provide positive attention and interest in the child's achievements.
- Robust, well-supported behaviour-management policies with an informed and united staff team in regular contact with the parents.
- Real celebration and reward for achievements both in improved behaviour and academic success.

Schools are often extremely creative and proactive in their attempts to engage disaffected children and should celebrate this. Outcomes are often hard to see in the short term and there is usually no 'quick fix'. Parents and staff members who are implementing policies and interventions need to be reassured that they are making a difference.

 Case study: Luke, aged 12

> Luke is a child with ADHD and Asperger's syndrome. In his first year at secondary school, he did well academically, but failed to make friends due to his outbursts of rage and disruptive behaviour when working with some staff members. He found breaks and lunchtimes particularly difficult. By the end of his second year, several interventions had been tried and failed, and his academic work was suffering. His mother and stepfather reported that his behaviour at home had deteriorated and that he regularly hit his mother.
>
> A meeting was held with all parties concerned including the SENCO, home/school support worker, parents, form tutor and deputy head. A plan was drawn up to help Luke, including a referral to CAMHS, a lunchtime supervision plan and one-to-one sessions with a specialist teaching assistant. Luke's parents were put in touch with a support group and attended a 'parenting your teenager' group with the home/school support worker. Luke was also given a peer mentor and attended regular group sessions with him.

Points for practice

This case study once again illustrates how encompassing a plan focusing on the whole family can be. The school team in this case concentrates on a programme to support Luke throughout the school day, including break times. He is also referred to CAMHS so that he can receive counselling regarding his anger and aggression.

The home/school support worker was able to provide information for the parents and work alongside them in improving their parenting skills. The goal was the same for the school and the home/school worker. It had been recognized that in this case Luke's behaviour and attitude would not be improved long term unless support was also provided for his mother and stepfather. By working alongside different professions, a holistic approach to issues can be effectively supported and managed.

Making a positive contribution and achieving economic well-being

Frequently for both child and family, those with serious anger and behavioural problems are disempowered by the system within which they are trying to function. In extreme cases, the child is permanently excluded from schooling, and support for the family is reduced to whatever the local authority has provision to offer. Other help must be requested and accessed by the parent, and if they have no knowledge or experience of what is available, or do not bother, then the child may spend months without any help or access to education. Outcomes for children in these situations are often poor. Many may have already experienced multiple crises or poor parenting, rejection, family break-up and addiction. The origins of the behavioural difficulties may never have been addressed and the child may feel responsible and hopeless.

To turn this around and begin to give a child and his family power to play an active and positive role in their own lives and that of their community is not an easy task. It should begin by consulting with the child and family and giving them ownership of some of the solutions to the problem. If solutions are merely imposed upon them, then it is unlikely that they will work. If, on the other hand, they have contributed to the plan of improvement, then they have a greater stake in ensuring its success.

Identification

Powerlessness and isolation affect children in different ways. The child may describe themselves as 'lonely', having no friends, or stupid and useless. The family may be socially isolated with other problems of poverty and destitution. There may be issues around social inclusion with families from ethnic minorities, troubled families, refugees and housing difficulties as well as the child's behaviour. There may be other siblings with behavioural problems. If a child is already isolated and socially excluded, the motivation to conform is already compromised. One eight-year-old child with serious emotional difficulties described his career ambition as wanting to 'pick apples' to earn money. He had a mother who was a prostitute and a disabled grandfather and had been seriously neglected all of his life. He was very able, but often depressed and sad, once stating that he was 'not looked after by anyone'.

Signs of social isolation include:

- Friendship problems, either in inappropriate choices or lack of friends.
- Behaviour motivated by a need to impress a peer group, showing off, appearing tough.
- Failure to access any extracurricular activities, clubs, sports, etc.
- A poor ability to cope with social situations, change of routine, etc. leading to outbursts of anger or inappropriate behaviour.
- Children who don't volunteer to take part or to help and are never picked for responsible jobs.
- Poor parental contact.

Once identified, these symptoms form a part of the overall problem of behavioural difficulties experienced by the child, both causing and resulting from their problems with behaviour. They may also help the school to identify other underlying problems of social deprivation, family problems and learning difficulties that might be driving the behavioural difficulties. It is all too easy to conclude that the behaviour is the problem and not acknowledge causation in other areas of the child's life. And whereas these causes may be intransigent, forcing interventions that address the behaviour as it presents, acknowledging them may in itself help: 'We understand that you are angry because your father has left home, but we still need you to deal with your behaviour in school'.

Interventions

These interventions focus on involving the child and family with the solutions to the anger and behaviour issues and helping them to contribute to their wider school and local community. They do not address the behaviour itself but should be seen as part of a behaviour-management strategy. One child became better, experienced a boost in her self-esteem and standing with peers when her mother succeeded in getting a job. Her behaviour and learning improved at this time and she started talking more about what she would like to be when she grew up. If a parent at primary level becomes involved as a school helper or member of PTFA, then children see and appreciate the interest and are given a positive example.

There are many ways in which parents and children may be encouraged to take a more active role in their lives and the wider community. Parents need to be supported in developing a greater involvement with their child's education and, through this, greater understanding about behavioural problems can be achieved. The following are ideas to help develop this relationship between the family, the support worker and the school:

1   Parental involvement in meetings concerning the child's behaviour. Supporting the parent at these meetings may involve a home/school support worker accompanying them, assessing their concerns beforehand and ensuring they have opportunities to speak, seeking clarity for the parent during the meeting and helping to explain outcomes afterwards.
2   Close home/school contact during the implementation of any plan to support the child gives parents the opportunity to voice their concerns and celebrate their successes frequently, preventing any little issues becoming a negative influence.
3   Child involvement in their behaviour improvement and opportunities given to the child to fully discuss their difficulties. Group work such as anger management with celebration and acknowledgement within the school for their successes, e.g. certificates presented at assemblies.
4   A separate acknowledgement and encouragement of talents and skills that is independent of the behaviour management, so that they do not easily lose the privilege of attending a sports club or drama group.

Involvement in the wider school and contributing to school events and successes can be encouraged by:

- allowing appropriate and carefully managed responsibilities
- identifying strengths and encouraging staff to involve the child

- listening to parents' ideas for their child; they know them best and will know what their out-of-school interests are
- home-based interventions to encourage parents to become more involved with their community. Inviting parents to use their knowledge and skills to benefit the community.

Any interventions that encourage and promote parental independence and involvement will in the long term benefit the child. These interventions may include support to return to work, encouragement to attend groups and meetings, and support to study or retrain. Children whose disaffection with education is due to behavioural difficulties are often also unable to function in a work environment and have little qualifications to allow them to proceed with further education. Their outcomes for economic well-being are therefore compromised and their long-term future is bleak. Early intervention is imperative to prevent these outcomes and should involve multi-agency approaches tailored to the child's needs.

Multi-agency working

Serious behavioural problems in children often involve a wide range of agencies including: CAMHS, attendance and behaviour service, educational welfare (Education Welfare Officers (EWO)), primary intervention projects and, where other problems are involved, Social Services, police, local addiction services and health teams. Where services have not previously been involved, a parent should be given clear explanations of what that service can offer the child and why the referral should be made.

Some services will become involved automatically as a consequence of the problem. The police service and EWOs fall into this category.

The EWO visits a school regularly and advises staff on those children who are failing to attend, are late or are absent without good reason. Schools will refer the family and the EWO will make contact. Police involvement may follow a criminal offence or complaint.

Supporting parents in dealing with these agencies may require a home/school support worker to explain clearly the nature of their involvement and what statutory powers they have. Where emotions are high, parents often fail to understand or remember what has been said to them in a meeting. Where parents are involved with decisions about their child, they are more likely to carry them through and support the intervention in school. Where parents understand that those involved are working for the benefit of the child with clear aims and attainable outcomes, they are more likely to support them.

Some areas of the country have well-developed **primary intervention projects** or **teams**. These are designed to address social, emotional and behavioural problems at what is classified Tier 1 and 2. At this level, agencies such as Social Services and CAMHS are not yet involved. They aim to intervene early to prevent further problems and deploy a multi-disciplinary team to most appropriately meet a child's needs. Teams may work through school referrals, health or parent self-referral and may offer help with parenting, emotional/mental health issues, anger management and social exclusion.

School nurse teams accept referrals for many Tier 1 and 2 issues and will also work with children in school who have referrals to higher tier agencies. They will address health (both mental and physical) problems and work with the child and the wider family members. Issues addressed include dietary problems, physical growth and puberty, sexual health, addiction and minor health issues.

Health visitors are very useful contacts for home/school support workers especially in early years work, because they have had involvement with the family for a long time prior to the child entering school. They are often well aware of the family problems and may be working with parents still where there are younger siblings. They also become important where there are sexual health issues and with teenagers who have become pregnant.

Social Services and **CAMHS** deal mostly with children with identified social or mental health needs at Tiers 3 and 4. These could be children in care or on the child protection register; children with Attention Deficit Hyperactivity Disorder (ADHD), eating disorders, or an autism spectrum disorder. In these circumstances, schools are still dealing with their day-to-day management and parental support at meetings and new implementing strategies may be necessary.

For children at risk of exclusion with SEN and Additional Educational Needs (AEN), local **Parent Partnership Services** may provide clear guidance on a parent's legal rights to appropriate education for their child and support parents through meetings with local authorities or courts. This is a service that local authorities are to offer, and provides independent parental support, and advice.

Adult education services offer the most consistent parenting courses and can structure them to suit the needs of the parents you are serving.

There are many other non-statutory agencies and charities offering help with parenting and behaviour management and some useful contacts are included at the end of this chapter.

Points for practice

With children whose behaviour is of serious concern, there are issues that workers should bear in mind around health and safety. These fall into two categories:

1 personal safety and protecting workers, other children and the child themselves from physical harm
2 protecting workers from accusations and from having to make impossible decisions.

Where workers are trained to handle a child who is likely to cause injury to themselves or others, then clear guidelines as to how and when this should happen, if possible involving the parents beforehand, should be drawn up. If the child is also made aware that if (a) happens then (b) will follow, this may go some way to preventing (a).

Preventing accusations and dangerous or awkward circumstances should be part of a safety plan where all those involved are clear about procedures. Management teams may feel it is not appropriate for a worker to be alone with a child; radios may be necessary for a worker to call for assistance in an emergency; other children may need to be briefed about evacuation of areas if a child is intent on causing harm. Safety procedures can never be 100 per cent effective, but can go a long way towards reassuring workers that they are protected and valued.

Stress management is also an important part of dealing with children who are hard to handle. Specialist teaching assistants assigned to children who require constant attention and supervision will need breaks and respite. Home/school support workers dealing with highly stressed parents with extreme problems will require supervision and opportunities to discuss their feelings. Many parents who have responded angrily during a crisis will apologise afterwards, citing frustration and desperation as reasons for their feelings of resentment. This is not surprising as, after all, it is they who have to cope with the child for the longest periods of time.

Dealing with parents who are feeling desperate, angry and frustrated by their child's behaviour and facing the prospect of possible exclusion requires tact and patience. Having a quiet and private room is important. Balancing the seriousness of the consequences of the child's behaviour with reassurance of school support can go some way to help parents remain calm. Ensuring that if a worker feels threatened by a parent they do not interview alone is good practice.

Summary

As can be seen in this chapter, there are many issues that may need to be considered as a result of the social, emotional and behavioural difficulties of a child. The home/school support worker will mostly focus on the needs of the family, but will nevertheless work towards the same goal as a school, that of the successful learning and social inclusion of a child. This chapter, particularly, also highlights the dangers, both physical and mental, that need to be carefully considered when working practices for a home/school support worker are being formulated. It is vital that the protection of all parties is carefully considered at all stages of a plan. It is no good planning for a home/school worker to meet regularly with parents in their home if, for example, a relative is aggressive or a consistent drug-user. Such a plan could put many people in physical danger. The employer has a clear role and responsibility to ensure that the safety and working practices of a home/school support worker remain within a professional framework. Home/school workers should not become friends (at least during an active piece of work) with the families they are working with, but should hold in mind at all times that they are a facilitator and part of a professional team.

〰️ Points for reflection

1   Reflect on a method you would use to help you consider issues that could be influencing/impacting on the social, emotional and behavioural needs of a young child. Draw up a simple five-point outline of what you would do when first asked to support such a child in a school.

2   Why do you think that the involvement of the whole family is essential? Do you think a school should still try to work with a child with social, emotional and behavioural needs if parents/guardians refuse support? Why?

3   Working with angry families can be extremely draining. How would you ensure that you did not become emotionally exhausted if working in this way?

4   If already working in a school, draw a spider diagram with the telephone numbers/contact details of all the agencies mentioned in this chapter. How well do you utilize their expertise and resources? Could this aspect of your work be improved or developed further and, if so, what additional help would you require to enable this to take place?

 Further reading

DfES (2004) *Improving Behaviour and Attendance: Guidance on exclusion from schools and pupil referral units.* Annesley: DfES.

 Useful websites

Behaviour 4 Learning – www.behaviour4learning.ac.uk

DfES, *Tackling it Together* – information about guidance and legislation on attendance and behaviour management – www.dfes.gov.uk/schoolattendance/publications/index.cfm

Government information about Parent Partnerships – www.direct.gov.uk/en/Education AndLearning/Schools/SpecialEducationalNeeds/DG_10016184

National Parent Partnership Network – www.parentpartnership.org.uk

National CAMHS Support Service (NCSS) – www.camhs.org.uk

Role of Social Services – www.teachernet.gov.uk/wholeschool/familyandcommunity/childprotection/otheragencyroles/socialservices

School Attendance Legislation – www.dfes.gov.uk/schoolattendance/legislation/ index.cfm

Teachernet (Education Welfare Service) – www.teachernet.gov.uk/management/atoz/e/educationwelfareservice

Young Minds – www.youngminds.org.uk/camhs

7

Coping with Addictions within the Family

In this chapter, the provision of support for children and families facing addiction, with its associated issues and anxieties, will be discussed. This will demonstrate how work carried out by the home/school support worker can have a positive impact on pupils' social and academic achievement in the long term.

Drug and alcohol misuse and addiction may truly be said to be a hidden epidemic causing grief and misery to many families coping in relative isolation. Once identified within a family, it often appears to explain many other problems for which it may be the root cause. Children suffer poverty, neglect, mental health issues, domestic violence and crime as a result of its impact.

The different types of addiction and their effects will be explored in this chapter, and the interventions and responses to children who are misusing substances will be considered. Addictions to gambling and internet chat rooms which have increasingly been coming to the attention of practitioners working with families will also be considered.

Every Child Matters

Within a household where a family member is affected by addiction, responses will vary from toleration and accommodation to rejection. The effect of the addiction will depend very much on the structure of the family and the person or persons misusing substances. Where one parent is addicted, the other parent will make hard choices about tolerating or confronting them and those choices will impact on the children and their ability to learn and cope socially. Where both parents are addicted, or in single-parent situations the lone parent is affected, then the outcomes for the children may be bleaker with neglect being commonplace. If a sibling is affected, the household suffers anxiety, conflict and crises as parents struggle to respond and cope.

One of the most telling aspects of addiction-affected households is the weird balance between a kind of coping and lurching between crises. Children may be seeing outbreaks of serious violence, overdoses and emergency hospital trips, police raids, criminal violence and robbery. They may be sleeping poorly due to night-time activities in the house, have a poor diet, be caring for themselves and younger siblings, keeping secrets and holding friends at arm's length. Through all this, outcomes will depend on resilience factors in their family circumstances, their own character and in the help offered through school, extended family or local organizations.

Being healthy

In a family where one or more family members are addicted, the following health risks for children may occur:

- Health is compromised through secondary effects of addiction, such as risk of violence, poor diet and poverty, neglect and lack of adequate sleep.
- Health is at risk because of exposure to illegal substances, alcohol, cigarettes and through poorly managed households with fire, sharp implements, etc.
- Health may also be at risk because children are exposed to adult behaviour affected by alcohol or drugs and may be supervised by adults who pose a risk to them.

Where children themselves are addicted or experimenting with illegal or dangerous drugs, risk factors include:

- Health affected directly by the use of the substance, e.g. cannabis posing a threat to their long-term mental health, excessive alcohol use causing damage to liver and other organs.
- Health risks through loss of control and inhibitions resulting in dangerous risk-taking.
- Loss of control, leaving children vulnerable to abuse by adults or other children.
- Risk of illness and injury due to contamination of needles etc.

There is another major area of health risk to children growing up in these circumstances and this is that their mental health is often affected by anxiety and uncertainty, social isolation and low self-esteem.

Identification

Signs of families affected by addiction are multiple. Children who are misusing substances should be identified if at all possible and this should be done through relevant training within school and in conjunction with health agencies. Within schools, information about a child abusing substances may come from peers or siblings and be clear and uncompromising. The only issue may involve adults failing to taking the warning seriously. Training in many schools is generally inadequate and many staff do not feel confident enough to identify and intervene in this area. Involving appropriate outside agencies may therefore be crucial.

While many families affected by addiction show signs of distress which could have a number of different causes, there are some indicators that should not be ignored:

- Self-referrals are the most important, either by a parent/carer or relative or by the child.
- Clear local knowledge of what is going on in a household where sources are trustworthy.
- Police or other agencies communicating with schools.
- Other signs, such as parents/carers appearing incapacitated or 'high' when they pick up a child from school or attend an appointment; a parent regularly smelling of alcohol at any time of the day.
- Children demonstrating age-inappropriate knowledge of drugs or talking about addiction to friends and staff.
- Sudden changes in behaviour/health or unexplained deterioration in academic achievement. This should always be investigated as there may be many serious reasons for such a decline.

Where secondary signs of neglect or abuse are present, knowledge of addiction as a cause may be forthcoming through interagency referrals, where another agency has contact with the family because of substance abuse.

Interventions

Many of the interventions in this area must be multi-agency and may involve referrals and close working with the school nurse service, CAMHS, local addiction support services, GPs, Social Services, police and health visitors where younger children are involved.

The multi-agency approach should persist whenever there are meetings about the child. Useful interventions for home/school support workers to support this approach include:

- A good relationship with the child/ren concerned with opportunities to talk in confidence about any problems or worries.
- Regular monitoring of disclosures and health status to spot any decline or crisis.
- Good education in areas of health, not just for children affected, but for the whole school.
- Good staff communication and training.

 Case study: Paul, aged 13

Paul is an only child; he has been a school refuser for two years. He has lived with his father's addiction to heroin all of his life, but three years ago he was alone with his father when he overdosed and Paul had to call an ambulance. There was no phone in the house and he had to run to several nearby houses before anyone would let him use their telephone. Since

(Continued)

(Continued)

then, he has seen his father overdose twice more and watches him constantly. He refused to go on school trips and has nightmares and difficulty sleeping. He began to find going to school difficult and would cry and become violent if he was forced to go. His mother disclosed his difficulties to the home/school support worker and she visited and spoke to both parents. Paul's father is now a registered addict seeking help and treatment though he frequently relapses. Paul is seeing a counsellor through his local CAMHS service and is receiving some home tuition. He hopes to start back at school next term part-time, but is worried about the schooling he has missed.

Points for practice

In this case, it is clear that without this support from the home/school worker, Paul may have permanently excluded himself from school. Responding to the mother's request, the worker was able to show to the parents how the father's behaviour and addiction were impacting on Paul's education and thus his life chances. This brief example only shows the start of the intervention, but hopefully with continuing support from the home/school support worker when he is reintroduced to school, Paul will be given the ability to cope with his feelings of fear for his father and also be positively enabled to deal with the amount of work he will be required to cover to 'catch up' with his peers. The school, the home/school worker, CAMHS, the parents and Paul will need to work together to ensure the plan is achieved.

Being safe

By its very nature, addiction of any kind does not allow a child to be completely safe. He or she is at risk at the very least from long-term emotional harm, living with levels of anxiety and uncertainty. Where the addiction causes violence or exposes the child to criminality, then risks of physical harm are considerable. A home/school support worker must consider referrals to police and Social Services through the school child protection team if they believe that the child is at risk of injury or abuse, and if the child's mental or emotional health is compromised. School child protection teams should have clear protocols for this eventuality and good links with Social Services and the police to enable efficient responses.

The realities of addiction are often that there is no long-term solution and that children will live with some threat all their childhood. Minimizing this risk is an important element of support for a child and can make a huge difference to their outcomes. One child who lived with an addicted father for many years would seek out a teaching assistant who knew her story and tell her whenever there was a crisis at home. Together, they would plan strategies to keep her safe and assess whether the family needed further help. On two occasions, they called in the child's mother and agreed a self-referral to Social Services.

Identification

The best way to identify children at risk, due to addiction in their family, is to give them safe and confidential channels of communication where realistic options can be discussed and where they can make sense of their lives through mutual support. This is particularly true of older children who may also be acting as carers for younger siblings and the addicted family member.

Children at risk of substance abuse may:

- show signs of other risk-taking behaviour
- already be smoking and drinking at an early age
- show changes in behaviour and health and a decline in academic achievement.

However, these children are most readily identified through peer or sibling disclosures, or their parents finding out. Parents may come with concerns about changes in behaviour, mood swings, secretive behaviour, etc. and not know the reason. These concerns should always be treated seriously and opportunities created for children to access the help they might need.

Interventions

Children in families affected by substance misuse may need any or all of the following types of support:

- Good support groups for children and parents and opportunities to discuss problems in confidence.
- Multi-agency working where possible with shared information.
- Regular reviews of the safety of the children concerned and appropriate referrals.
- Safety plans worked out with the children and parents/carers to anticipate emergencies and plan for them.

Children at risk of substance misuse may need any or all of the following:

- By far the most effective intervention to prevent the misuse of drugs in children is good education and opportunities to discuss and ask questions. Secondary schools often have well-developed PSHE programmes to tackle this, while primary education still needs to develop programmes.
- Peer support programmes to address peer cultures that tend towards substance misuse.
- Open channels for parents to seek help and advice from staff and other agencies; information about drugs and addiction available in school for parents to access.
- Communication with parents when there are concerns about changes in a child's behaviour or health.

Case study: Ahmed, aged 15

Ahmed is a refugee child who came to Britain from Eastern Europe, unaccompanied. He was intelligent and studious with family who phoned him regularly and sent money. He has been housed with foster carers for four years. In the last two years, he has been meeting with other teenagers in his area and his behaviour and attitude to learning had changed. His foster carer suspected he was taking drugs, but he managed to hide the signs from her. One day, while she was cleaning, his foster carer discovered class A drugs in his room and the police were informed.

School was notified and his home/school support worker began liaising with police, Social Services and Looked After Children (LAC) agencies to provide some support in school for Ahmed to try and help him. He stated that he is ashamed of himself and that his family will be devastated. He wants help to clean up and will cooperate with the police. His foster carer is not sure if he is being truthful.

Points for practice

Whether Ahmed is being truthful or not to his carer and support worker, it is essential that he receive services that will help him to cope with the physical, mental and social issues he is going to have to face. With a multi-agency action plan in place, at least Ahmed will have the opportunities and support he will need to 'clean up' and to make the best of his educational opportunities. Ahmed is already an LAC child with regular meetings held to assess his needs. A multi-agency plan would include his LAC worker, Social Services, police, young offenders' team, school nurse service and addiction support workers, school support worker and teacher, his foster carers and Ahmed himself. Other services that may be involved include CAMHS, refugee or minority group support services locally, and local community or volunteer agencies. Regular communication between all those involved should be planned. Ahmed would be seeing several support workers for either individual or group therapy. His physical health will be monitored and his attendance and achievement in school encouraged. With Ahmed playing an active role in devising the plan and agreeing to abide by its terms, he is more likely to benefit from the help and support the plan offers.

Enjoy and achieve

Where children are living in a household that is affected by drug misuse or addiction, then one of their overwhelming feelings is constant anxiety. Where young children are concerned, then there may also be confusion and a poor understanding of what is going on, but older children will frequently understand the situation and keep secrets about what is happening.

Where addiction fuels domestic violence, poverty and neglect, poor housing situations and lack of academic support, then the effects on these children are similar to those we have discussed in the other relevant chapters. However, drug addiction in itself is a huge cause of concern to children and it is worth pausing here to consider children's opinions on the habits of their parents.

One child stated: 'I wish my parents wouldn't smoke near the new baby. My mum shouldn't smoke in the room with the baby.' (Boy aged 9)

Another, when asked about whether he enjoyed his summer holiday, said: 'No, all the grown-ups got drunk and had fights.' (Boy aged 10)

The daughter of an amphetamine-addicted parent stated: 'I want him to leave because he threatens us, but I'm worried about what will happen to him and where he'll go.' (Girl aged 12)

By secondary school, many social pressures to conform and be like your peers have forced children in these situations into silence and concealment. It is easier to say that you have a parent who is sick than addicted.

Interventions

Helping children to overcome the anxieties and concerns of living with addiction should be a consideration for schools, because so many children are affected in some way. Where that addiction is life-threatening, the child effectively lives with a terminally ill person and may be very well aware of this. One child with a father addicted to alcohol found him dead when she came home from school. There was no one else in the house at the time as her stepmother was working.

The following interventions may be useful for working with children affected by addiction.

1   To help these children, schools should seek professional advice and training. Where counselling is available through schools, this should be offered and where group support can be set up, staff members should be suitably trained. Links with local voluntary support agencies can also be forged through schools giving children options for accessing appropriate help.
2   Where home circumstances create a barrier to learning, mentors and home/ school support staff should be made aware and offer appropriate help, both pastoral and practical. No child should suffer because they cannot bring in money for trips or do not have the equipment to join in with activities.
3   Good channels of confidential communication should be offered.
4   Connexions and young carers' groups should be used to offer career and development advice and respite. Most local areas have young carers' programmes run by local charities and a list of web addresses is given at the end of this chapter.
5   Many children in these circumstances don't attend clubs or recreational groups because of difficulties with transport and money. Any practical help that allows them to access these facilities gives them a greater choice and allows them some real childhood experiences.
6   Referrals to other agencies, primary intervention projects, CAMHS, the school nurse service, etc. should be made where criteria are met. Schools should be up to date and efficient in these referral procedures to prevent delays.

Most of all, bear in mind the provision of opportunities for these children to look forward to a future that they themselves control. Points of failure along this route often coincide with transitions between schools and public examinations and this is where the help should be concentrated.

 Case study: Max, aged 13

Max's family is chaotic. He has four younger siblings by two different fathers and his own father is unknown to him. His mother and stepfather smoke and drink heavily. For his 30th birthday, his stepfather brought in ecstasy tablets and these were consumed with the alcohol most of the day. By early evening, the flat was chaotic and all of the children were in serious danger of accidents or consuming drugs themselves. All the other children were under 10 years old. Two were pre-school. At the end of this incident, the police were called when Max's stepfather became violent and then collapsed. He survived the effects of the drugs and alcohol and was arrested.

Max and three of his siblings were eventually taken into care. Multi-agency interventions were put in place to support the children, but there were still some serious consequences for Max's mental health and well-being.

At school, he was supported through transition to secondary school and was given a peer mentor to help him settle and make friends. He received counselling for several months and needed help again when he had contact with his siblings. He finds it very hard to stop worrying about them, as for so many years he was their most sensible carer.

Points for practice

The most significant point to remember from this case study is the issue that despite what many adults will tell them, children feel a deep sense of responsibility for siblings, who they may be caring for, and for their parents. In many cases, this is hard to understand, but it is vital to recognize that even months after the children are all well cared for, feelings of responsibility and loss will impact on the sibling who was the carer and protector of the family. If not dealt with sensitively and proactively, it can result in this child developing mental-health issues such as depression.

They will need long-term support in school to cope with educational and social challenges. They may well need long-term counselling or a mentor, especially at times of change or transition.

Making a positive contribution

School represents a unique environment for children living with addiction. Their own home circumstances may be chaotic with the added concerns and anxieties around the destructive or violent behaviour of the addict leading to a sense of powerlessness. In school, there can be consistent security with staff members aware and sensitive to these children's needs. There can also be reliable support when things go wrong and encouragement for achievement. Including a child in school makes them feel normal when most of their lives they hide the truth, avoid taking friends home, cope with illness and violence, and often care for an adult who cannot care for themselves. One child reported how her drunken father would come home and climb into her bed, smelling of drink and vomit. She would have to push him out and guide him to the sofa or give up her bed to him. She was 12 at the time and coming home from school to an empty house and caring for herself first.

Schools can provide an environment where children are listened to, are safe and find people to trust. Nevertheless, their home-life experience can leave them feeling isolated and uncared for. Isolation in children is characterized by:

- never joining in with any outside activities
- shyness and withdrawal
- embarrassment at the behaviour or appearance of their parents
- being victimized and bullied
- having no voice, no chance to talk about their ambitions or achievements.

Including these children should be a positive policy with direct targeting and encouragement. It is not enough to say that there are extracurricular activities available, that they could stand as school councillors if they wanted to or that they can't be persuaded to stand up and take part. Ways should be offered that are tailored to the child, encouraging him to take a more active role in his own school life.

Examples of ways in which these children and their families can be encouraged to contribute might include:

- Offering a mentor or dedicated support worker who is available to talk and can offer practical solutions to help a child fully integrate into his school life.
- Actively encouraging children to join in with school community activities. This may mean ensuring there is transport available to collect and return the children home or that they have the right clothing or fees. It may also require permission from home for the children to access activities, and the school or home/school support worker might facilitate this.
- Working to reward children and celebrate their achievements even if their parents don't turn up to appreciate their endeavours.
- Forming links with members of their family who can and will encourage and support them. Offering groups and activities for such families.

Achieve economic well-being

The Every Child Matters agenda aims to break the cycle of poverty and under-achievement that exists in some families. Where drug abuse or addiction is a part of that family's life, then there is a serious risk that the children in such families will grow up failing to fulfil their own potential and even repeating patterns of behaviour that are self-destructive. With intervention and support from relevant agencies and charities, family members who are supportive and education tailored to their social need, as well as their academic ability, the possibility of economic well-being could be realized. Addiction by its very nature damages the financial foundations of families, costing money to supply a demand and often leading to the incapacity of the addicted adult. Where the child is misusing substances, then the risk of long-term addiction and financial hardship is very great.

Gambling and internet addictions

While these types of addiction do not directly threaten health, they are a huge cause for concern within families because of the financial hardship they create. Gambling addiction can lead to serious debt and is another hidden problem with little acknowledgement of its true impact. Within schools, it can only be approached through concerns raised about the debt and poverty it may cause but home/school support staff may hold information on helplines and websites, local charities and agencies.

Internet chat rooms, games, etc. are a growing worry for many professionals dealing with family problems. Many children are being allowed unlimited access to hours of online amusements and the problem may not always be limited to children. Both these areas deserve further consideration and research to assess the true impact on children's education and prospects. Schools could facilitate ways to help parents address these concerns through IT courses and specialist advice on blocking sites. Schools could also provide information and advice to children on the dangers involved.

In the previous sections of this chapter, ways that support these children both practically and emotionally have been discussed. Their best chance of future economic well-being is through education and emotional support, building resilience factors that will enable them to create stable adult lives. Some of these children have tragic and fractured childhoods with little normality. The following example illustrates just how complex these problems can be and follows the life of one small girl, touching briefly and periodically with authorities that fail to bring any real stability or normality.

 ## Case study: Holly, aged 7

Holly is the eldest of six children. Her mother is addicted to class A drugs and her father is unknown to her. By the age of seven, Holly had three younger siblings and she and her mother had lived in five different houses or flats with three different partners. Holly was frequently left in charge of her younger sister and brothers while her mother was out of the house. Her mother would have friends round to their home, and this involved strangers drinking, smoking and taking drugs for most of the day and through the night. Holly's schooling by the age of eight had included six different primary schools and patches of several weeks at a time when she did not attend at all.

Her fifth school had a home/school support worker who found Holly in alone one day when the school had not seen her for several days and her mother could not be contacted on her mobile. Holly was 'minding' her two younger siblings while her mother took the baby out. Holly's mother regularly shoplifted to fund her drug habit. Social Services were informed and knew of Holly's mother from previous referrals. For a while, Holly's attendance improved, but a visit one morning by the home/school worker found the children left in the care of a male visitor who was drunk and asleep on the sofa. Holly's mother had been taken to hospital the night before with a miscarriage.

Soon after this, Holly's mother moved to another part of the country. She took Holly but the three younger children were taken to their father's and Holly's grandparents and left there. Holly didn't see them again for two years. Holly's mother had two more babies in the next two years. Holly went to four more schools. Both of the younger children were taken into care and Holly was left 'looking after' her mother whose health had by this time broken down.

Home/school support workers in several of Holly's schools passed on information about her and attempted to address her problems. Holly's schooling was so patchy that she was often left confused by the work in her new school. She was a keen and enthusiastic pupil when she did attend, but very shy. The authors do not know what happened to Holly in the long term.

Multi-agency working

Where a child is growing up with addiction in the home, the consequences for that child can be so severe that multi-agency intervention should be inevitable. In reality, the high numbers of children involved combined with the scarcity of professional workers and the difficulty in identifying families affected means that there are many children who grow up with little support, surviving the consequences of addiction as best they can. Equally, there are families where the addict is 'contained' and one parent manages the consequences of the addiction, holding things together as best they can. In other families, the addict may manage to break their habit and improvements are made followed by relapses and improvements as the struggle continues. Such families often don't access help available because of a failure to admit the addiction, ignorance of that help or a reluctance to let anyone know their problems.

A home/school support worker may be able to bridge the gap between the families in need in this way and the services available. Agencies set up to counter addiction will rely on Social Services for referrals and, while Social Services may be able to refer those families with acute problems, many families that manage some degree of normality and do not come to the attention of higher tier agencies are offered no help. If a child can be identified in school and a relationship of trust built up with the family, then involving other support agencies becomes a possibility. Specialist services can be put in place, support groups accessed and opportunities explored.

Working with these families is often a creative experience. The needs of any one child or family are never the same. There is help available, but it often does not reach those in greatest need or for whom a real difference could be made and matching the child or family with the opportunity is a challenge.

Where statutory agencies are involved with a family, there may be poor communication because a service will be provided for the adult that has no provision for linking up with services for the wider family or the children. An addict may have a mental-health worker, a social worker and a GP or consultant for their health problems, but these individuals may never meet and may never communicate with the children's schools or any agencies dealing with the welfare of the family as a whole. A home/school worker can take the opportunity to rectify this if they feel it could be helpful, and there is nothing to stop a school calling a multi-agency meeting and inviting all relevant professionals if they feel it could help the children.

 Case study: Susan

Susan is addicted to prescription medication. Her partner is a heroin addict and they have five dependant children between the ages of 7 and 15. They have real affection and concern for their children and will support them in many ways, but the family lurches between crises on a regular basis depending on the addiction and the financial circumstances of the family. Susan has recently begun to try to recover and has secured a part-time job. She failed to notify the benefits agency and has been threatened with court action. The family is very poor, managing on a low income and paying out for debts incurred over several years. The home/school support worker has known Susan for several years. He has liaised with the benefits agency, Social Services when they are involved, the police when the older boys have been in trouble, secondary schools to help with transfers and several charities. The local town has a St Vincent de Paul Society and he has applied for the two oldest children to go on a holiday with them. The family has also accessed a holiday together through a local charity. The children attend a young carers' group run by the local council and Susan is now going to a support group for recovering addicts. Her partner has been in hospital recently following an accidental overdose. He is being offered help through the local health trust to break his habit. The home/school support worker has had to find uniforms, food in emergencies, school shoes on a regular basis and equipment for games. He has good relationships with several statutory and non-statutory agencies that can provide help like this. Recently, he has encouraged Susan and her partner to tackle their debt problems with the support of the Citizen's Advice Bureau.

Points for practice

It could be very easy to be judgmental in cases such as this. However, it is vital that the home/school support worker remains focused on securing the best outcomes for the children involved at all times. In this case study, the home/school worker provided the following types of intervention:

- practical help for the children, e.g. clothing and equipment
- arranged holidays for the children through local charitable groups
- provided information and support to the mother
- encouraged the parents to tackle their problems, rather than trying to ignore them
- worked with other agencies involved with the family, such as the police and benefits agency
- worked with other schools ensuring transitions are as smooth for the children as possible.

General points for practice

Safety

Workers should be aware that addiction comes with inherent risks to those in close contact. Where a worker is visiting, risk assessments should be conducted bearing in mind physical risks from objects in the home, risk from unpredictable, aggressive or violent individuals, and risk from visitors to the home. One family kept large dogs of uncertain temper which prevented the home/school worker from visiting because she did not feel safe, despite the family's reassurances. It is the responsibility of the individual worker's line management to make sure that no undue risks are being taken.

Other points of safety to consider are the emotional impact of working with families where crises and tragedies may occur or where children are regularly put at risk or obviously suffering anxiety and harm. In these circumstances, it is wise to ensure that the home/school support worker has adequate supervision available. For those engaged in this work, doing your best and following good practice will never fully alleviate the difficulties of children in these circumstances, but may make a real difference in the future.

Confidentiality

Home/school support workers will find themselves working with families living with addiction where there is no clear acknowledgement of the position. The family does not want the situation widely known, the children do not want friends or members of staff to know and there may not even be an admission of the true nature of the problem. In other families where the problem is acknowledged, there *must* be a genuine respect for the privacy of that family while sharing the information with those who need to know and can help and being open with the family, seeking permission and informing them when contacts are made with other agencies. Most families are very willing for information to be shared in order to access help, but this must not be presumed and families must be consulted when any new contact is made.

Records about families should be kept securely and be available for scrutiny by the family should they request it.

As with every other issue, the child's safety is paramount and must not be compromised, so where a child is in danger parental permission is not required for referrals to the appropriate agency, although parents are still informed if this does not pose an immediate risk to the child.

Child protection

Child safety is obviously a serious issue where addiction is concerned and we have discussed how school staff should take seriously any disclosures of possible risk or injury (see Appendix 3). Because of the long-term nature of addiction, there are continuous risks, both physical and emotional, to children left in these situations. Schools have a unique opportunity to monitor these situations where they hold information about the home circumstances and home/school support workers can play a valuable part in this. It is good practice to maintain a relationship with parents and children in these circumstances even when there is no obvious need or crisis. It is more likely that parents will accept help and children will take opportunities to confide when times are hard if they have a clear and open channel of communication with a person they trust.

 Summary

This chapter has addressed the complex problems posed by substance misuse in families. It has considered children with family members who are addicted, and children experimenting with illegal drugs themselves. Through the case studies, the serious effects of addiction on the health, emotional and social well-being of children has been discussed. We have shown how addiction within a family can cause serious difficulties in all areas of a child's life including education and illustrated ways in which this might be alleviated through school involvement.

⌇ Points for reflection

1   It is vital that you reflect on your own views and experiences of addiction. It will not be possible to work effectively with others who have an addiction until you examine your own views and confront any prejudices or fears.

2   Remember that drug addiction is only one of many addictions and that in society today there are many addictions that can impact on children's outcomes. How do you think a child may be affected who

lives with a parent who has a gambling addiction? How would you try to support this child and the family?

3   Assessing risk is a vital aspect of this type of work. Why do you think it is vital for a home/school support worker to carry out a risk assessment for each home visit? Discuss with a colleague if possible.

4   Consider carefully to which agencies you would first refer if you and the parents knew that a child was addicted to drugs or smoking. Do you think that this support will need to be short or long term? Why?

Further reading

Barnard, M. (2007) *Drug Addiction and Families*. London: Jessica Kingsley.

Useful websites

Community Care – www.communitycare.co.uk/Articles/2007/07/05/105042/drug-addiction-and-families.html

Connexions – www.connexions-direct.com

Gamcare – www.gamcare.org.uk/publications2.php/Books.html www.gamblersanony-mous.org.uk and www.addictions.co.uk

Support for young carers can be found at the following websites:

www.barnardos.org.uk

www.bubblycrew.org.uk (Hammersmith and Fulham)

www.carers.org

www.carersuk.org

www.nch.or.uk

www.svp.org.uk

www.youngcarer.com

Mrs Yvonne Durkan Children's Camps UK
Tel: 01634 375413
Email: ydurkan@hotmail.com or brentwood@svp.org.uk

8

Working Directly with Children

> Many home/school support workers are involved in providing input for children through individual or group activities within the daily curriculum timetable. This requires a whole range of different skills, a different kind of relationship with a child and will lead to different career opportunities and experience. Child-based interventions such as transition work, one-to-one support, listening and understanding will be discussed in this chapter.

If the purpose of school is to educate the child, then many of the roles we have discussed in this book so far are about overcoming barriers to learning and enabling a child to engage more fully with their education within school. Those barriers may stem from a child's social background and be due to poor parenting, poverty and neglect, cultural and language difficulties arising from migration and travel, learning difficulties and many other life circumstances. Within schools, attempts are often made through individual or group working to help the child to overcome some of these difficulties and here we will explore how this can be best achieved. School staff engaged in this work are often teaching assistants and pastoral support workers; they will frequently be asked to work from published programmes with the support of a SENCO, specialist teacher or outside agency. The work itself could be around self-esteem, anger management, behaviour issues, friendship and social skills. Good training and line management is essential if this work is to be successful. Poorly delivered and ill-judged pastoral support may well do more harm than good.

In this chapter, we will consider the practice of working with individuals and groups within school, rather than the content of programmes. We will look at the structuring of these interventions and the liaison with parents and carers.

Every Child Matters

Despite our best efforts to ensure every child is taught in a manner that recognizes the individual's own strengths and weaknesses, busy schools will often

prove, due to pressures of time and financial restraints, to be prescriptive, forcing uniformity and routine. While robust and well-supported children may
cope well with this most of the time and inform us when they are struggling,
many less fortunate children will find managing a school day and learning, a
near impossible task. Such difficulties may be transient – a bereavement or family breakdown, for example, or they may be chronic – addiction or neglect leading to years of faltering education. If a school structures its pastoral care to
provide a strong support network with opportunities for children to take part in
small groups and individual pastoral sessions, then a culture of caring develops
and children learn to access help without embarrassment or fear of ridicule. The
pastoral care can then extend to pupil involvement groups, forums and councils, peer mentoring and friendship groups, and form part of the career development of all the pupils within the school. The five outcomes of the Every
Child Matters agenda become an integral part in the culture of the school where
difficulties are met with strong teams and tried-and-tested solutions.

The National Healthy Schools Programme identifies four areas: personal,
social and health education (PSHE), healthy eating, physical education and
emotional health and well-being. Each of these play a part in engaging and
supporting children in school, but the first and the last will provide the focus
for this chapter, within the framework of ECM.

Being healthy

Parents and schools aim to nurture mature young people whose attitude to
health is balanced and responsible. The challenge for schools within PSHE
frameworks is to ensure that all children in the school become interested in
their own health, are knowledgeable about health matters and are realistically
aware of the risks to health when they make choices about behaviour. Schools
may quickly identify children who are vulnerable in this area and small group
work or individual support can greatly enhance a child's chances of achieving
a healthy lifestyle.

Identification

Children identified as vulnerable may include:

- those from socially deprived family backgrounds
- those with a known history of risk-taking or substance misuse
- those with poor dietary habits
- those with poor exercise habits
- those with a diagnosed medical condition or disability.

Individual work

Once identified, individual children in need of support may be referred to outside agencies, receive support from other health professionals, receive counselling or have parent and family work offered. A pastoral support worker, aware
of the needs of the individual child, promotes full engagement with the services
offered and provides daily support in school. A child being seen by an eating
disorder clinic, for example, may wish to regularly drop in to the pastoral

support worker for reassurance and confidential guidance. Structured time for this may allow a child to work through practical issues around coping with the school day, managing lunchtimes, and avoiding destructive peer groups. Examples of individual work include:

- supporting a child to keep a food and drink diary to show her clinic nurse
- working through barriers to taking part in PE
- supporting a child with a chronic medical condition or disability; giving them a chance to express their own views on their condition and any difficulties they are experiencing.

Key to the success of this work is the contact with parents and other professionals whenever this is safe and relevant. Close teamworking with family and other agencies ensures a continuity of support and a wider understanding of the child's entire requirements.

Supporting a child in the understanding of diabetes or ADHD will need good knowledge and judgement of age-appropriate explanations. It is worth considering here why this type of work should be undertaken in school, while medical and health professionals hold the knowledge and see the child in a medical setting appropriate to answering questions. If a child suffers from a chronic health problem and grows up with it, their understanding of what is wrong with them will depend upon their age and development. While explanations will be given to the child at various stages, usually during their clinic appointments, many children outgrow these explanations before they are updated.

Misunderstandings arise and confusions may abound and the child will express those confusions at odd times often to parents or other adults who have care of them. In school, situations will arise that convince a teacher or other school professional that a child is not coping with a disability or a chronic illness on an emotional level. A child will frequently ask questions about this and seek answers from adults he feels safe with. A staff member with good contacts with healthcare professionals and parents may be able to supply answers to these questions in a setting favourable to the child.

The following is an example of this type of situation. A child with a physical disability in a mainstream secondary school was frequently concerned about the fire drill in school. He was always helped to leave the building, but was aware that his progress was slow and that some areas of the building were harder to exit than others. When he expressed this concern to his parents, his learning support worker was able to talk him through his worries and the local fire and rescue service sent a disabled community liaison officer to speak with him.

Group work

Small group work may well centre around health issues including:

- healthy eating, cookery and nutrition clubs
- targeted group work aimed at children with specific problems, e.g. reluctance to exercise, obesity, poor eating habits, drug misuse (stopping smoking programmes), sexual health, etc.
- gardening and alternative exercise programmes

- providing opportunities for children to talk about issues raised in PSHE where those issues have a direct bearing on their lives, or are causing them worry or anxiety.

While schools will include in their PHSE curricula programmes to tackle many of these issues, identified children may still benefit from working within a small group in order to better understand the problems they are facing.

At primary level, the interventions around health may include those children who are reluctant to engage in physical activity in the playground. Some really simple work can be done with children who don't want to join in competitive sports or fast physical games, but can benefit from nature walks, outdoor activities around conservation and gardening, dance clubs and small group sports.

Where poor dietary habits are a problem, support workers have set up dinner clubs that allow children a quieter and more structured lunch break than the communal lunch hall. For some children, sitting around a table with adults is a new experience and children can be taught to tackle food they haven't tried before.

Home/school support workers have worked in conjunction with school nurse services and other health-care professionals to set up groups for children who smoke and misuse alcohol, and with the right support schools can provide safe forums for such groups and support changes in life choices.

 ## Case study: Kara, aged 10

Ten-year-old Kara, who had been diagnosed with diabetes when she was seven, began manipulating her eating to gain adult attention and absence from class. In a one-to-one conversation with her home/school support worker, she was found to have little understanding of her condition above what she had been told at seven.

Points for practice

The home/school support worker referred Kara to a specialist diabetes nurse. She was then able to be given a more age-appropriate explanation of her condition, making her more aware of the risks she was taking and more careful of her own health. Having the time to make contact with specialist services and to talk at length to children thus allows appropriate input to be given by professions at the time they are required, preventing adverse behaviours developing and unnecessary health risks.

 ## Case study: Sadie, aged 10

Sadie has been overweight since she was first in school. She was identified as obese by the school nurse after a referral from the home/school support worker, Leslie, in conjunction with Sadie's mother when Sadie was in Year

(Continued)

(Continued)

5. Sadie's mother, Pearl, is concerned about her daughter going to secondary school and being bullied for her size. Pearl does not seem to recognize the health implications for Sadie and feels she will grow out of her weight problem. All Sadie's family are overweight.

Sadie began seeing the home/school support worker in school whenever she felt depressed. She began helping with a walking club that was set up to encourage children who did not like competitive sports. The children and two adults have a one-hour walk with a rest halfway once a week after school. Sadie helped Leslie make posters for this.

Leslie also encouraged Sadie to keep a food diary for a week to show the school nurse and then encouraged Pearl to take Sadie to her clinic appointments. Sadie worked with Leslie writing down all the things she finds it hard to cut down on, particularly chocolate, and they thought of ways in which Sadie could try to be strong.

By the time Sadie reached Year 6, she had lost some weight, but constant and consistent support has been vital to keep Sadie and Pearl focusing on the issue of healthy eating.

Points for practice

Obesity in a young child can have long-term social, emotional and health implications. In this case study, Sadie was experiencing depression and concerns were already being raised about the risks of bullying in secondary school, due to her weight. It was essential that the home/school support worker worked with Pearl as well as Sadie, because of the need for cooperation required at home. Despite a lot of input from the home/school support worker and the clinic, this clearly requires long-term input. Pearl had not really taken on board the risks to Sadie that obesity can cause and thus work needs to continue until this is achieved. The significance of the parents not really wanting to change and improve the situation is very clear in this example.

Being safe

There are two different sets of circumstances that expose children to risk of harm:

1   unsafe environments in the home or community
2   lifestyle choices that pose serious risk.

While unsafe environments, neglect and poverty have been addressed in Chapter 5, it is worth remembering here that good mentoring systems and individual encouragement and support for such children may provide the resilience factors necessary to overcome their hardship and may be crucial in identifying children at risk of serious harm.

Tackling the effects of destructive behaviour through challenging peer groups and providing alternative role models can be an effective means of turning a child's behaviour around. Where problems are acute, input from and collaboration with specialist workers with a good knowledge of local communities may be required. The involvement of youth services, such as Connexions, local youth clubs, police youth offending and prevention teams and groups dedicated to tackling specific problems may also be advantageous.

However, even in schools where extreme problems are rare or isolated, much good work can be done with dedicated members of staff trained to facilitate group discussions, circle time, peer support groups, peer mentoring and student councils. Many children fall into problems through ignorance and a desire to gain status within a group. Providing sound information about the inherent dangers of certain behaviours and alternative ways to meet and make friends can change the culture of the school and prevent dangerous behaviours.

Anti-bullying

Bullying represents a specific threat to the safety of a victim, both physically and mentally, and tackling bullying is a subject constantly raised by government and schools. Robust anti-bullying policies, clear procedures for reporting and clear sanctions for offenders will help schools proactively deal with bullying. It is not enough for schools to show that they react to bullying when it comes to light; they must presume bullying occurs and act to promote a school community that does not condone or tolerate it.

Providing specific adults who can be approached and who will never be too busy to listen and believe the children is an important strategy for preventing serious bullying. A staff member who gets to know the children and understands those who will exaggerate and attention-seek, and those who are reluctant to speak up compensates for faults in communication. They will also encourage children to support one another and promote a genuine culture of respect.

Identification

It is worth referring here to previous chapters where children concerned are at risk of substance abuse, neglect or criminal behaviours. Bullied children often manifest with similar anxiety-driven symptoms. More general identification of children at risk of harm from bullying must rely on good staff reporting and adults who are willing to spend time listening. Children themselves often know when a friend or classmate is at risk. Where indicators are small but persistent, 'drip' reporting can be used with a class log or a system of forms for staff members to pass on their concerns to the child protection team (see Appendices 1 and 3). Clear protocols about the confidentiality, regular reviewing, storing and shredding of these must be drawn up and staff training kept up to date on their use (see Appendix 5).

Interventions

Small groups designed to tackle bullying, risk-taking behaviour and safety must include peer development, as many such problems arise within groups. Some well-tried group work includes:

- circle work
- peer mentoring schemes
- friendship groups (e.g. Circle of Friends)
- anti-bullying, self-esteem and social skills groups.

Enjoy and achieve and making a positive contribution

Wherever possible, children should enjoy their educational experience and through this learn to fully engage with the positive aspects of academic achievement. Children identified as failing in education, at risk of exclusion or disengaged with the process of learning need help to begin to enjoy their schooling. Even small achievements can be celebrated and give rise to an improvement in self-esteem.

Identification

When considering children who fail to achieve and appear deeply unhappy with the learning process, wide differences in presentation may be noted. Such a group will include:

- children identified as having behavioural problems who will often think very poorly of themselves, describing themselves as 'thick' or 'stupid' and feeling genuinely separated from their achieving peer group
- children with learning difficulties where those difficulties are not properly identified or catered for
- children unable to keep up with their peers due to poor parental support
- children who feel isolated for cultural or language differences or because of physical appearance or presentation
- children with a specific fear or worry that blankets all other achievements, e.g. bullied children.

Low self-esteem runs through these categories making school feel like a deeply humiliating and stressful experience.

Interventions

As has been clearly illustrated throughout this book, child-centred interventions should involve the full commitment of the parents, giving them opportunities to encourage their child and voice their opinions on progress. In the following suggestions to improve self-esteem therefore, it is taken as read that parents will be informed and encouraged to contribute in any way they can. Home/school support workers may:

- hold small group work sessions around self-esteem and self-image
- support the appropriate streaming and setting of work to match ability and clear identification of difficulties
- provide and support peer mentoring
- arrange adult mentors – this may simply be a different member of staff whom the child respects who can show interest in the child's achievements and to whom they can go with difficulties or successes

- organize a work folder where exceptional pieces of work can be stored over time and where a child can look back and see the progress he has made
- facilitate the close liaison with parents, which may include providing parents with stickers and achievement certificates to mark their child's successes
- help to develop a whole school emphasis on rewarding achievement and effort to include those whose successes are small.

However, it must be remembered, as mentioned in Chapter 7, *that the child's needs are paramount and must not be compromised at all.*

While all of these things are good tools to address poor achievement and unhappiness in school, they should be used with a clear understanding of the specific needs of an individual child. For example, some children may be too shy to accept 'centre of attention' praise, while others may be so aware of their deficits in comparison to their peers, that seeking out and finding a school 'role' for them that celebrates their unique talents may work best. If we aim to create within our schools a community where everyone has a role, then no child should feel left out or unable to achieve.

 ## Case study: Margo, aged 6

Margo is struggling with school due to specific learning difficulties and chronic shyness. In group work, she is unable to join in verbally and often says nothing at all. Her mother is concerned about her ability to enjoy school because she is always so anxious. Her class teacher has encouraged Margo's mother to come to school as a helper once or twice a week. This has helped Margo feel special because her mother is helping other children. The home/school support worker runs the school council and Margo's class elected her as a member. At first, she was too shy to speak at all, but after several sessions and with the help of another child, she began to join in with the votes non-verbally and express opinions quietly when every member was asked.

Points for practice
Margo's shyness is only a problem if it is impacting on her happiness, ability to learn and join in. Margo's mother raised concerns and is the referrer. The home/school support offered here comes first from the teacher who is Margo's mother's first contact, and the teacher and the home/school support worker are part of the same team helping Margo to achieve in ways that are tailored to her needs and take into account her feelings.

Achieve economic well-being
The two clear aspects of this Every Child Matters outcome are the current economic well-being of the child's family and the child's own future prospects of

economic independence. The most vulnerable families may have experienced several generations of poverty and reliance on benefits, and the expectations of the children may be extremely low. Groups at particular risk of long-term poverty and disaffection with education may involve:

- children whose parents have poor literacy and numeracy skills
- families with a history of educational disaffection, including traveller groups, unskilled workers and the long-term unemployed
- chaotic families suffering successions of crises due to illness, poverty, housing difficulties and social breakdown
- excluded children and school refusers
- children with additional or special educational needs where there is poor parental support and understanding of the difficulties they face.

All of these groups suffer or are at risk of suffering economic hardship and supporting children in such groups provides an opportunity to improve their long-term life chances.

Interventions

Interventions that encourage and support financial independence in young people will necessarily be focused on secondary education, particularly the 14–16-year-olds. However, earlier work around practical skill, self-esteem, transition to secondary school and communication skills is always very useful. Secondary level intervention should recognize that some children, however gifted, will fail to reach their full educational potential at school, and encouraging them to leave with skills that will enable them to make a living and an understanding that learning can be lifelong is a good compromise. Interventions aimed at enabling children to be independent adults include:

- any trips or visits that broaden their experience and encourage wider social interaction
- alternative curricula designed to develop talents and skills for practical work experience
- an involvement with local businesses, services and industries or with local colleges and universities
- good use of Connexions and other careers and youth services
- peer mentoring schemes from the wider community
- support for applications and interviews, particularly where this is not forthcoming at home.

General points for practice

Confidentiality

Real professional confidentiality requires self-discipline and vigilance, particularly in a busy school. When a support worker is asked to speak to a child who is experiencing difficulties, the first thing the referrer will do after the intervention is to ask what was said. While we acknowledge that counselling is confidential when conducted on a professional footing, we may be slow to protect the confidences of children in a less formal environment.

Simple rules for disclosures in confidence are:

1. Clearly inform the child that you will keep anything they may tell you in strict confidence unless it relates to something where they or someone else may be in danger of harm, or unless they have asked you or allowed you to tell someone.
2. Respect all confidence, no matter how trivial or amusing.
3. Make a clear statement to other adults or children asking questions that you will not tell them because it would not be right.
   NOTE: Where disclosures are made to a worker about violence or abuse and a child has been told rule 1, you can be reasonably sure that the child wishes you to tell others and is genuinely asking for help.

Keeping to these simple rules ensures that the school community comes to recognize the privacy of such interventions and to trust in a worker's judgement and integrity. It is very easy in school to be drawn into conversations that are speculative and where you hold privileged information on a child. **Respecting a confidence must apply even when others already appear to know a particular fact**.

Parental notification

Parental notification is not always necessary before a child is seen if the support worker is a member of staff and all parents are clear about their role with children. However, if a child is to be included in a specific group for a particular type of intervention then parents should be notified and, in practice, parental support and involvement in such work is almost universally beneficial. Rules of confidentiality still apply to parents, but if a worker feels a parent (or other relevant adult) ought to know about a particular problem, then the child can be asked if they would allow such a communication to be made.

Personal safety

Working with small groups of vulnerable children, or one to one with no other adult present may require a risk assessment (see Appendix 2). If any of those children are likely to threaten harm or become unmanageable, it should be possible to call for assistance. Some schools have personal radios or restrict work to rooms that have phone links. A senior management awareness of working practices should be clear where safety is a concern.

Preparation and evaluation

Social skills groups, anger management and other small group work require the same level of careful preparation as more academic work. Support workers should receive the correct training and management support for this work and should be prepared to evaluate what they have done. Group work can be informal on a drop-in or drop-out basis as the need arises, but the intervention itself should be regularly reviewed to ensure it is effective.

Where a child has a pastoral support programme or other individual plan, then the report and evaluation of the intervention should be included in their records. The following case study demonstrates how good planning focusing on the needs of an individual child can actually enable him to begin to positively access learning and education in school. Working with an engaged parent, using the young person's interest and strength can help attendance and motivation. The home/school worker also needs to evaluate a programme of support step by step, ensuring that the next step planned is still in the correct direction.

 Case study: Adam, aged 14

> Adam has a long history of school refusal and disaffection. He comes from a family where his mother is an alcoholic and his father is illiterate. He is the youngest of six children and most of his older siblings have not achieved well at school. His parents have moved house several times and Adam was never adequately cared for. His experience of school to date has been one of constantly being ill-prepared and appearing neglected. It was easier for him not to attend.
>
> Through his home/school support worker, a relationship has been established with his father who works as a gardener with the local parks authority. Adam was placed on an alternative curriculum programme with his local youth worker and given a tutor for three hours a week. His tutoring sessions took place in the youth club where he felt safe. Social Services were engaged to try to promote better household arrangements and things improved when Adam's mother moved in with his older sister. Adam has now returned to school on a part-time basis to attend practical courses and basic literacy and numeracy lessons. He is thinking more positively about his future and often goes to work with his father. He sees a Connexions worker every month. The home/school worker helped them to apply for an allotment and they now work on this together.

Points for practice

Adam's problems are long term and intervention should aim to address them in the long term. Connexions and the local youth service will help Adam through the remainder of his schooling and beyond. The home/school support worker first established a working link with Adam's father who is his effective parent and worked with him to engage with Adam. Good liaison with other support agencies will help Adam with his transition from school into further education or the work place.

Summary

This chapter has shown how a home/school support worker may be utilized within the school curriculum, facilitating direct work with children. This type of work is not always expected or wanted within a school community, but where skills or time are lacking within the teaching staff team, then a well trained and dedicated home/school support worker may be accessed to provide this level of support.

 Points for reflection

1   Do you feel that direct working with children within the school day is/should be part of a home/school support worker's role? Write a list of factors which support such work and one which rejects this view. Evaluate the answers given.

2   Reflect on when children need help to cope with learning and the school community. Should the support required within school be provided by the same person/team that is responsible for home liaison work?

3   What skills and qualifications are necessary, do you think, for home/ school support workers to support children within the mainstream curriculum?

4   Consider whether you feel that a support worker could experience a conflict of interest if he works with school staff and a child and also the family who are perhaps causing the difficulties and anxieties for the child. Discuss.

Further reading

School–Home Support (2006) *Crossing the Boundary from Home to School.* A summary report for parents, carers, children and young people involved in the School–Home Support Isle of Dogs project. London: School–Home Support. Also at www.school-homesupport.org.uk/Publications/Researchsummaries

School–Home Support (2006) *Working with Parents: Forging links between school and home that enhance children's experience of school.* London: School–Home Support. Also at www.schoolhomesupport.org.uk/Publications/Workingwithfamilies

 Useful websites

National Children's Bureau – www.ncb.org.uk

National Healthy Schools Programme – www.healthyschools.gov.uk

School–Home Support – www.schoolhomesupport.org.uk/Home

9

Moving Forward

> This book has been written to meet the needs of an increasing number of school-based support staff who are engaged in the pastoral care of children and their families. They provide a vital link between home and school, encouraging the involvement of parents and supporting families through difficulties and crises. This work aims to keep children as fully engaged with their education as is possible and reflects the desired outcomes of the Every Child Matters agenda.

The development of home/school support has been sporadic across the counties with some areas far in advance of others, particularly in inner cities. Roles are very varied and offer support to communities on a needs basis, encompassing migrants and travellers, ethnic minorities and language groups, preschool, primary and secondary schools, disadvantaged groups and Looked After Children. It is only in very recent years that central government has begun to take notice and to introduce pilot schemes, placing parent support advisers in schools, while individual schools, local government and local children's funds have been steadily supporting this development in certain areas of the country for several decades.

While central government is proceeding with its 'Every Child Matters' and 'Every Parent Matters' agendas with extended schools and Children's Centres foremost in its sights, local authorities and individual schools have proceeded with their own home/school support projects on the basis of tackling deprivation and underachievement. However, home/school support workers did not come into post to provide community learning, out-of-hours' clubs and holiday play schemes. They were mainly instigated to address poor outcomes for certain groups or local areas, and the means may have included what are now classed as extended schools activities where these have proven to be effective. They might just as easily involve walking-buses, parent forums, school-based intervention groups or individual home visits. Where government is picking up the baton and imposing its own agenda on all schools, then some conflict may arise and these opposing forces must be reconciled if the roles are to be successfully developed.

Reconciling roles

Government policy states:

> The delivery of the Every Child Matters agenda will involve widespread initiatives across a number of sectors to ensure coherence in children's services. Extended schools will be at the heart of this delivery. We are also confident that the principles of workforce remodelling, if appropriately applied, should enable schools to identify the appropriate skill-set for those involved in the development and delivery of extended services.

> Where school support staff have the relevant skills and experience and wish to be involved in the new opportunities which emerge from extended provision, this should not be to the detriment of their existing duties and may have implications for their pay and grading. (DfES, March 2005)

The Extended Schools Prospectus (DfES, June 2005) sets out the core services that schools should provide by 2010. Among these services are parenting support and information, particularly at key transition points, family support for those whose children have special needs of any kind, and adult learning opportunities and advice. Extended Schools are seen as places where parents can access help within a familiar community setting and children and families can be supported in times of crisis. Children's Centres also have a similar remit to the Extended Schools, but for parents and children under five: 'The purpose of a Children's Centre is to reduce child poverty and social exclusion ... and to provide inclusive services that are responsive to local community needs and preferences' (Cheminais, 2007: 14). This is important to remember as the parents with children attending mainstream schools may also have children under the age of five. Therefore, there may well be a need for professionals from Children's Centres to work alongside and collaboratively with workers in schools. This work falls naturally to the duty of existing home/school support staff and where new posts are being created, responsibilities for the delivery of such services can be a designated part of the role.

Children's Centres are a multi-agency environment with a clear need for good liaison with school staff to ease transition and engage with new parents. A home/school worker may play a crucial role, meeting with health visitors to be informed of families where additional support may be needed, liaising with play groups and nurseries to provide information to parents and alerting school staff to community welfare needs and concerns. Where this model is being applied, the role is proving invaluable.

However, existing staff have a wider variety of roles that have included support for individual pupils in a variety of child-centred and school-based interventions. These may be small group work with children experiencing emotional difficulties, playground support, individual mentoring, transition support and many more. While some staff are clearly differentiated by their role as learning mentors or school-based pastoral support personnel, it can be argued that there is a place for a worker who does both school-based, child-centred work and parent contact and support. In this capacity, the support given to the child is not seen in isolation and the family is treated holistically. Many problems have been solved by simple practical solutions worked out between the child, the parent/carer and the school. If government policy forces schools to choose to redefine the role of the home/school support worker in line with the Extended Schools agenda, so that they concentrate entirely on parent support, then a vital and valuable model will be lost.

It is important to remember that home/school support should be as broad and varied as the communities they serve and there is room for many models of employment. Many schools have limited funding for these posts, while others have developed models that split the role providing pastoral support for children from one worker and home/school support with another. In these situations, good teamwork is essential to ensure that home-based concerns are addressed and holistic solutions are delivered.

Long-term support

One of the strengths of the school-based role is its continuous nature. In so many other areas of intervention, there is an emphasis on completion and closure, successfully bringing a case to a conclusion where intervention can be withdrawn. In part, this is due to a false premise that families should be able to survive without support from professionals and that the ideal family is independent and free from crises. Because of this, families living with long-term chronic problems cycle between periods of intervention from Social Services and health professionals, specialist education and mental health support, and withdrawal when things are improving. In reality, the help should remain in place through the better times, bringing at least a possibility that the cycle might be broken and a hope that some of the problems might be alleviated. School-based home/school support roles have the potential to address these issues because they are by nature continuous and concerned with the day-to-day management of children in education. Workers are far more likely to pick up on early signs of distress and head off serious crises, and they are more likely to develop relationships with parents that allow them to ask for help before circumstances deteriorate. Importantly, they are also around to celebrate and encourage small successes as and when they occur.

With consideration of all the areas of need discussed within this book, it is extremely clear that a family coping on a low income with two children with learning difficulties and a chronically ill adult is permanently in need of support. Short-term intervention periodically withdrawn is not going to change the life of a single mother with four very young children living in poverty with no family support. These parents are simply doing a job that should not be attempted by one person on their own. The potential for breakdown and crisis is enormous and parents living with these difficulties are often carrying personal problems that make them even less able to cope. Their only real hope of a brighter future is in more consistent help over many years, providing practical solutions, somewhere to talk, adult education opportunities, guidance through official channels and links with other agencies that can help. It is logical that this help should happen through pre-schools and schools, because it is these establishments that aim to provide a better future for the next generation of parents by supporting and encouraging the children. Raising expectations and increasing children's internal ability to cope with social and emotional issues cannot be accomplished quickly, but needs consistent and meaningful progressive work. Children and parents need to build relationships and to learn to trust and feel safe within an environment before any real change can be achieved.

Social workers in school versus parent support and advice

During the past few years, Social Services have been developing relationships with home/school support workers, taking advantage of the close contact they have with vulnerable families. A model has developed where home/school support workers take an active role in supporting children who are designated Child in Need or are on the Child Protection Register. Schools have always played a role in meetings and core groups (key professionals tasked to directly support the family) as part of multi-agency working. However, with the advent of Children's Services replacing separate education, health and Social Services provision, this is seen as a growing responsibility. With a designated home/school support worker as a part of the school staff, it is natural for schools to use this person as a core group member and to include them in meetings. Through their regular contact with the family, they are familiar with ongoing problems and can monitor the progress of the family on a weekly basis.

This particular aspect of home/school support can be extremely stressful and involves taking decisions about personal safety, child protection and family support. It may involve accessing emergency funding and after-hours working with families in immediate crisis. While social workers are subject to regular supervision and support, professional appraisals of risk and clear guidelines as to what action to take, schools have no such historical infrastructure. Such posts are usually line-managed by the head teacher, deputy or SENCO, with the initial understanding that the individual worker will liaise with parents to sort out minor problems. Any school, particularly one in a deprived area, will carry a caseload of several families who are either designated Social Services cases or should be. The home/school support worker risks becoming an unofficial social worker to these families and one who works without adequate support, financial and professional recognition and supervision. Concerns around schools' ability to cope with this and the long-term effects on the worker should be raised and discussed regularly.

As an important part of the development of the post, school staff who undertake this kind of work should be acknowledged to be doing so, supported and supervised adequately and paid appropriately. If the model of a Tier 1/Tier 2 'social worker', working through schools with a small caseload of specific families or working on general preventive work with families facing crises of various kinds, is a valid one then it should be affirmed, adequately funded and supervised. Social Services have become more aware of the potential of this level of preventive work and there are schools that have a social worker officially designated to fulfil this role. This, in itself, raises the question of job descriptions and workloads if a single individual can be paid to cover the 'social work' part of home/school support while other school-employed workers attempt to cover this and several other roles (extended and health schools, parent adviser, small group work, etc.).

To conclude, anecdotal evidence from schools and from home/school support personnel has shown frustration and anxiety about the conflict between Social Services' cases and broader educational support for families. Home/school support workers are not trained, supported or paid to be social workers in school and if this proves to be a desirable model of working, then these specific areas should be addressed.

1　Home/school support workers should be adequately trained to hold low-tier cases.
2　Social Services should support and acknowledge that schools are holding potential Child in Need and Child Protection cases and meet regularly to discuss them.
3　Home/school support workers should be supported and supervised in this role within the school and health and safety issues should be addressed.
4　Home/school support workers' pay and conditions should reflect this type of working and other demands on their time should be reduced to allow them to fulfil this role properly.

Data handling

Confidentiality is an integral part of working practice for all school staff and home/school liaison is a particularly sensitive area. Practice and training should include sound protocols for handling data including diaries, day books, individual case records and contact details. Such records enable workers to keep track of brief contacts, phone calls and requests for information during busy working days, and schools must provide adequate secure storage both for hard copies and computer records. This can and should be integrated into existing school record-keeping, with sensitive information on individual families being kept separate from children's records and shredded or wiped when no longer required. If a worker is to be trusted by families, then they must be involved and informed about the storage and handling of their personal information. Data sharing with other agencies should be with the consent and understanding of families unless child protection issues prevent this. An easy reference for workers to ensure good practice is to question at all times whether the information is kept and shared in the best interest of the families and with their knowledge and understanding. A wider debate and consideration of this area would be welcome.

Confidentiality and sharing of information within schools will have to be considered as home/school support and Extended Schools become more widespread. If staff members are to be involved in supporting families through sensitive times, then they must be cautious about who they share information with and how they discuss cases with staff members. If Extended Schools mean parents and other members of the wider community are present in school, then this raises further issues about protecting data. Again, these considerations require a wider discussion and clear procedures and guidelines for schools.

Evaluation and value for money

Where budgets are committed to funding a person for a specific task within school, then evaluation must take place at some stage to ascertain the impact of such work. There are several levels to this that need to be taken into consideration:

- Evaluation of the individual doing the job through line management as part of performance management. This can be invaluable for school senior management – because of the independent and unique working of home/school support within school, they can often be unaware of precisely how much is being done and in what areas.
- Evaluation within school as to the impact of a home/school support worker on attendance, behaviour, parent involvement and educational achievement.
- Evaluation by funding authorities on the impact of home/school liaison across communities and broader local areas. This may be quantitative, looking at educational outcomes and families accessing local services, or qualitative, gathering information on school staff's attitudes to home/school support and family appreciation of the support they have received.

The work is hard to evaluate quantitatively because of the long-term nature of the interventions and the progress resulting from them. Furthermore, the work is by definition preventative, addressing problems early on and seeking to prevent crises, so like all such work it may not always be measurable in any positive terms, i.e. this family did not need Social Services' involvement because the home/school support worker was able to access help with debt before they were made homeless.

Current research being undertaken may show positive effects that can be attributed to home/school support roles in the next generation of school children.

Working conditions and pay

The newness of the home/school support role within many areas may lead to some problems integrating and supporting a worker within a school. We have spoken earlier about health and safety, stress and isolation (Chapter 1) and, in future, schools should consider ways to integrate and support a worker within the staff structure. Particularly important are lines of communication, not just for the worker to pass relevant information to staff and receive referrals, but also for the worker to be included in school events and news.

Pay structures at present are determined locally and home/school support staff are paid what schools and local authorities can afford. Many are on short-term contracts with retention subject to central or local funding being renewed every few years. Pay does not often reflect years of service, training and experience or responsibility, and frameworks for promotion are poor. Where workers are undertaking stressful and arduous work with families, there is little parity with colleagues in Social Services or health and this lack of career opportunity is reflected in the nature of the workforce. Positions are often part-time and poorly paid and are largely occupied by women returners to work, young people beginning in caring professions, or those seeking part-time and term-time work due to family commitments. While the work is rewarding and demanding, the opportunities to stay and develop a career are not good and many experienced and devoted workers will leave for other opportunities when their circumstances and qualifications permit.

If central government and local authorities seriously believe that home/ school support is the way forward and is valuable in tackling poverty, disaffection and unemployment, then a greater commitment to those undertaking the role should be made. Without such a commitment, the projects will be compromised; able and experienced workers will leave as other opportunities arise, newly appointed workers will require training, and the full benefit of a well-structured career with good worker retention will never be fully realized. Home/school support will remain a patchy experiment in social change, never fully funded or committed to and subject to the policies of successive governments. Despite the insecurity and poor pay, most workers find the role deeply satisfying and rewarding and would continue if they could.

Future planning for this role needs to give greater weight to the needs and qualifications of employees. If initial evaluations prove the role to be valuable and this seems to be the case at present, then more status should be given to those working in the field. Where individuals have proved themselves invaluable to the working of the school, solving problems that have created barriers to learning and easing the burden on teaching staff, then schools have independently found the means to retain them and reward them. This model should be recognized and funding should be more secure and structured.

Supervision, networking and support

As mentioned throughout this book, there are stresses and difficulties inherent in dealing with families with problems. In allied caring professions, work of this nature is supervised with clear structures to allow workers to discuss and seek peer support. Where possible, home/school support staff should receive such support either in school or within school clusters with other similar workers. Where such models have been tried, workers feel valued and are given opportunities to support one another. Just as other school staff (SENCOs and subject coordinators, for example) find value in networking with colleagues from other local schools, home/school support workers derive huge benefit from peer support of this nature. Many local schools share families and problems, services and resources, and networking meetings allow workers to share general information and offer advice to one another. This is a valuable practice and should be appreciated and encouraged.

To conclude, many home/school support personnel have worked for many years in communities that appreciate and value them. They have experience and wisdom in dealing practically with problems that beset families on a daily basis, both minor and overwhelming. They need to be recognized and rewarded, given security and career opportunities that allow them to continue what has proved to be valuable and rewarding work. This quiet experiment has earned a higher profile through local successes and achievements. Those individuals engaged in the work deserve more security and a celebration of their success.

Bibliography

Chapter 1

Department for Education and Employment (1995) *Protecting Children from Abuse: The role of the Education Service.* Circular 10.95. London: DfEE. www.dfes.gov.uk/publications/guidanceonthelaw/10_95/summary.htm

Department for Education and Skills (2003) *Every Child Matters*, Green Paper, CM5860.

Department for Education and Skills (2004) *Every Child Matters: Change for Children*: DfES/1081/2004.

Department for Education and Skills (June 2005) *Extended Schools: Access to opportunities and services for all – A prospectus.* Annesley: DfES. http://teachernet.gov.uk/eOrdering Download/1408-2005PDF-EN-01.pdf

Department of Health (2000) *Assessing Children in Need and their Families: Practice guidance.* London: TSO. www.dh.gov.uk/en/Publicationsandstatistics/Publications/Publications PolicyAndGuidance/DH_4006576

Department of Health (2001) *Children's Social Services' Core Information Requirements.* Process Model Version 2.0. London: The Department of Health. www.dh.gov.uk/en/ Publicationsandstatistics/Publications/PublicationsPolicyAndGuidance/DH_4007556

Department of Health *(2002) Working with Children in Need and their Families: Draft consultation document.* London: The Department of Health. www.dh.gov.uk/en/ Publicationsandstatistics/Publications/PublicationsPolicyAndGuidance/DH_4005215

Department of Health (May 2007) *Birth to Five.* London: NHS. www.dh.gov.uk/en/ Publicationsandstatistics/Publications/PublicationsPolicyAndGuidance/DH_074924

Department of Health, Department for Education and Employment and the Home Office (2000) *Framework for the Assessment of Children in Need and their Families.* London: TSO. www.dh.gov.uk/en/Publicationsandstatistics/Publications/Publications PolicyAndGuidance/DH_4003256

HM Government (2006) *What to Do if You're Worried a child is Being Abused: Every Child Matters, change for children.* Annesley: DfES. www.everychildmatters.gov.uk/_files/ 34C39F24E7EF47FBA9139FA01C7B0370.pdf

HMSO (2004) *Children Act 2004.* London: TSO. www.opsi.gov.uk/acts/acts2004/ 20040031.htm

HMSO (2006) *Working Together to Safeguard Children: A guide to inter-agency working to safeguard and promote the welfare of children.* London: TSO.

Home Office (May 2004) *Working within the Sexual Offences Act 2003, SOA/4.* London: Home Office Communications Directorate.

National Offender Management Service (July 2005) *Probation Circular: 54/2004*, Issue 1.0, Reference No. PC54/2005. London: National Probation Directorate. www.probation.homeoffice.gov.uk/files/pdf/PC54%202005.pdf

Chapter 2

Brecklin, L. (2002) 'The role of perpetrator alcohol use in the injury outcomes of intimate assaults', *Journal of Family Violence*, 17(3): 185–97.

Cleaver, H., Unell, I. and Aldgate, J. (1999) *Children's Needs – Parenting Capacity: The impact of parental mental illness, problem alcohol and drug use, and domestic violence on children's development*. London: TSO.

HMSO (1989) *Children Act 1989*. London: TSO.

HMSO (2002) *Adoption and Children Act 2002*. London: TSO.

Kershaw, C., Chivite-Matthews, N., Thomas, C. and Aust, R. (2001) *The 2001 British Crime Survey: First Results, England and Wales, 18/01*. London: HMSO. www.homeoffice. gov.uk/rds/pdfs/hosb1801.pdf

Mullender, A., Hague, G., Imam, U., Kelly, L., Malos, E. and Regan, L. (2002) *Children's Perspectives on Domestic Violence*. London: Sage.

Mullender, A. (2004) *'Tackling Domestic Violence: Providing support for children who have witnessed domestic violence'*. Home Office Development and Practice Report online publication: www.renewal.net/Documents/RNET/Policy%20Guidance/Tacklingdomestic violencechildren.pdf

Chapter 3

Childhood Bereavement Network (2006) *A Guide to Developing Good Practice in Childhood Bereavement Services*. London: National Children's Bureau.

Graham, P. and Hughes, C. (1997) *So Young, So Sad, So Listen*. London: Gaskell.

Job, N. and Frances, G. (2004) *Childhood Bereavement*. London: National Children's Bureau.

McAuliffe, A-M., Linsey, A. and Fowler, J. (2006) *Childcare Act 2006*. London: National Children's Bureau.

Mosley, J. (1998) *Quality Circle Time in the Primary Classroom*. Wisbech: LDA.

Ribbens McCarty, J.R. with Jessop, J. (2005) *Young people, Bereavement and Loss: Disruptive transitions?* London: National Children's Bureau.

Chapter 4

Centre for Studies on Inclusive Education (CSIE) (2002 revised) *Index for Inclusion: Developing learning and participation in schools*. Tony Booth and Mel Ainscow, Bristol: CSIE.

Department for Education and Skills (2001) *Special Educational Needs Code of Practice*. Annesley: DfES.

Newton, C. and Wilson, D. (2003) *Creating Circles of Friends*. Nottingham: Inclusive Solutions.

Soan, S. (ed.) (2005) *Additional Educational Needs*. London: David Fulton.

Tutt, R. and Barthorpe, T. (2006) *All Inclusive? Moving Beyond the SEN Inclusion Debate*. Devon: The Iris Press.

Chapter 5

Department for Education and Skills (2006) *Safeguarding Children and Safer Recruitment in Education.* Annesley: DfES.

Desforges, C. and Abouchaar, A. (2003) *The Impact of Parental Involvement, Parental Support and Family Education on Pupil Achievement and Adjustment: A literature review.* Research Report 433. Annesley: DfES.

Wilkin, A., Kinder, K., White, R., Atkinson, M. and Doherty, P. (2003) *Towards the Development of Extended Schools.* NFER Research Report 408. Annesley: DfES.

Chapter 6

Department for Education and Skills (2004) *Improving Behaviour and Attendance: Guidance on exclusion from schools and pupil referral units.* Annesley: DfES.

Chapter 7

Barnard, M. (2007) *Drug Addiction and Families.* London: Jessica Kingsley.

Chapter 8

Cheminais, R. (2007) *Extended Schools and Children's Centres: a practical guide.* Oxfordshire: Routledge.

Chapter 9

Cheminais, R. (2007) *Extended Schools and Children's Centres: a practical guide.* Oxfordshire Routledge.

Department for Education and Skills (2001) *Special Educational Needs Code of Practice.* Annesley: DfES.

Department for Education and Skills (2003) *Every Child Matters.* London: TSO.

Department for Education and Skills (2004a) *Removing Barriers to Achievement: The government's strategy for SEN.* Annesley: DfES.

Department for Education and Skills (2004b) *Every Child Matters: Change for children in schools.* Annesley: DfES.

Department for Education and Skills (March 2005) *Raising Standards and Tackling Workload Implementing the National Agreement,* Note 11. Annesley: DfES.

Department for Education and Skills (June 2005) *Extended Schools: Access to opportunities and services for all – A prospectus.* Annesley: DfES.

Department for Education and Skills (2005) *Education Improvement Partnerships: Local Collaboration for School Improvement and Better Service Delivery.* Annesley: DfES.

Department for Education and Skills (2006) *National Audit of Support, Services and Provision for Children with Low Incidence Needs.* Research Report 729. Annesley: DfES.

Desforges, C. and Abouchaar, A. (2003) *The Impact of Parental Involvement, Parental Support and Family Education on Pupil Achievement and Adjustment: A literature review.* Research Report 433. Annesley: DfES.

Ofsted (2005) *Inclusion: The impact of LEA Support and Outreach Services* www. ofsted gov.UK

Rogers, R. Tod, J., Powell, S. Godfrey, R., Graham-Matheson, L., Carlson, A. and Cornwall, J. (2006) *Evaluation of the Special Educational Needs Parent Partnership Services in England.* Research Report 719. Annesley: DfES.

Wilkin, A., Kinder, K., White, R., Atkinson, M. and Doherty, P. (2003) *Towards the Development of Extended Schools.* NFER Research Report 408. Annesley: DfES.

Appendices

If you go to http://www.sagepub.co.uk/digman you will be able to download PDFs of the material included in this Appendix.

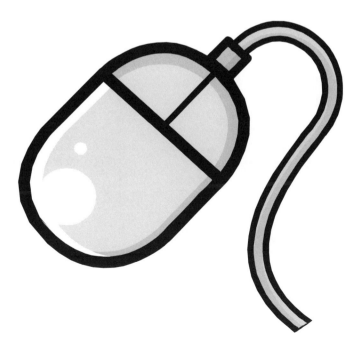

CONFIDENTIAL Referral to home/school support team/worker	
Name of child: Class/year group:	
Request for action: (e.g. please contact parent regarding issue)	Nature of concern: (e.g. despite several attempts, parents of this child are not contactable on phone and do not reply to letter. Child has been left in school after hours for up to 15 minutes on several occasions and picked up by older sibling)
Name of referrer:	Feedback to referrer:

Photocopiable:

Working with Parents © Carmel Digman and Sue Soan, 2008

Appendix 2
Protocol for Worker Safety When Visiting and Interviewing Parents

1 Schools should possess a clear risk-assessment policy for any staff who are working alone or visiting families. Risk assessment should be conducted before each new visit or contact.

2 Designated members of the senior management team should be responsible for overseeing staff safety in these situations. All staff should be aware of procedures.

3 When visiting or meeting a parent/carer off-site, the worker should notify a designated staff member of their intentions, whereabouts and the duration of the meeting.

4 General safety rules should be followed at all times.

5 Always carry a mobile phone. Consider having someone call you to check the visit is going well.

6 Think about exiting a situation. Can this be done easily should the need arise?

7 Consider the area in which you are meeting as well as the person. If in doubt, arrange to meet in a known safe place like a café or social centre.

8 Consider visiting with a colleague.

9 Consider all manner of dangers including environmental risk (broken bottles, needles, smoking, etc.), dogs, other family members or friends of the person you are visiting, unlit stairways and corridors, parking arrangements.

10 If you are in doubt, don't go; don't be ashamed of telling your management team you are uncomfortable with a situation.

NOTE: More detailed information on personal safety is available from The Suzy Lamplugh Trust.

 Photocopiable:

Working with Parents © Carmel Digman and Sue Soan, 2008

Appendix 3
School [name] Child Protection Slip

Number.................

An informal record of staff concerns about a child; designed to contribute to an ongoing cumulative record.

Child's name:
Referrer:
Concern:
Date: Signed:

Further action taken:
Feedback to referrer:

Appendix 4

Protocol for School: in the event of a sudden death or serious injury of staff member, child, parent or significant adult, or member of wider community

The school recognizes the possibility of such an incident and in such a situation would put the following procedures into place:

1   Following such an incident, the head teacher would first inform the staff and then the whole school at a special assembly. Children would be told factually what has happened and given the opportunity to pray.

2   The senior management will assess the seriousness of the incident and the extent of the reaction necessary.

3   Trained members of staff would be identified to offer support to children at designated times of the day. Designated areas would be set up for quiet reflection and accessing adult support.

4   The head teacher or other senior manager will deal with any media requests.

5   Local CAMHS and Educational Psychology teams will be notified.

6   The pastoral support team (home/school support worker/s) will offer support to the family concerned and keep in touch with the head teacher regarding progress in this area.

7   The senior management team, in consultation with the family, will decide on attendance at the funeral, memorial services, etc.

8   Long-term support will be considered for all children and adults affected.

9   Local community/religious leaders will be consulted and involved where this is appropriate to the needs of the school community and the wishes of the family.

10 In all things, the family of the deceased should be considered and consulted.

 Photocopiable:

Working with Parents © Carmel Digman and Sue Soan, 2008

Appendix 5
Child Protection Protocol for Home/School Liaison Workers

This protocol is not a replacement for school child protection procedures and should rather be seen as an additional policy for staff working in close contact with families.

1 All staff, including designated home/school support workers, should be aware of the school child protection policy and procedures. They should be aware of the lead Child Protection Officer in school and should meet regularly with him/her to discuss any concerns.

2 Decisions on referrals to statutory authorities (Social Services, police) should not be made by the home/school liaison worker, but by the designated CP Officer. Home/school support personnel should not hold the CP Officer role.

3 Home/school support personnel should be fully CP-trained by the relevant local authority and this training should be regularly updated.

4 Home/school support personnel should be ready to support parents making self-referrals to statutory authorities in the event of CP concerns.

5 Where home/school support personnel are accompanying parents to CP meetings, they should not be the sole representative of the school. A senior teacher/SENCO should also be present to support the school's position from an educational perspective.

6 Home/school support personnel should keep accurate, dated notes on their support for families with CP concerns as part of the school's system of monitoring at-risk children. These notes should be kept securely according to school data handling procedures.

7. Where possible and safe, home/school support personnel should work closely with family members to ensure the safety and educational needs of the children concerned.

8. Home/school support personnel should be aware of health and safety procedures at all times. They should be adequately supported and supervised when dealing with CP cases.

Schools may choose to modify the protocol depending on the terms and conditions of the home/school support worker's contract. This is a general guideline only.

 Photocopiable:

Working with Parents © Carmel Digman and Sue Soan, 2008

| Home/school support Networking Meeting |
| **[NAME OF LOCAL SCHOOLS' GROUP]** |
| **[DATE]** |

Group members present/apologies:

Invited visitors present and agencies they represent:

Issues discussed:

Useful contact details for visiting agencies:

Appendix 7
Policy Statement and Practice and Procedure Guidelines Safeguarding and Protecting
the Welfare of Children (including Child Protection)

Note: This is a sample policy only that includes a great deal of detail and, as such, it will incorporate information that may well not be appropriate for all schools to include in their child protection policies.

Policy statement

It is the policy of .... that there will be an absolute commitment from staff to the physical, emotional, sexual and spiritual well-being of the children/young people at the .... Others accessing the school's services will also be protected from any form of harm, neglect or abuse. The school's child protection procedures have been developed in accordance with Safeguarding and Protecting the Welfare of Children Guidance 2006 and the principles established by the Children Act 1989, Care Standards Act 2000, Sexual Offences Act 2003 and Children Act 2004.

Alongside this policy statement and practice and procedure guidelines focusing on safeguarding and protecting the welfare of children, staff are also asked to read the following policies and practice guidelines which are designed to ensure the safety and well-being of the children/young people in our care as well as the staff:

- Anti-Bullying Policy
- Complaints and Representations Policy
- Missing Children Policy
- Administration of Medication Policy
- Relationships and Sex Education Policy
- HIV/Aids Policy
- Physically Holding Children – A Guide to Practice
- Behaviour Management Policy
- Lone Working Policy.

Safeguarding and protecting the welfare of children (including child protection) – policy statement and practice and procedure guidelines

Child protection principles

- Staff working with children/young people will, at all times, act as responsible adults and maintain an appropriate adult/child boundary and relationship (Personal/Professional Boundary Policy).
- Staff will respect a child/young person's right to express themselves and only restrict his or her liberty to do so if there is a risk of significant harm as outlined in our Physical Restraint Policy.

- Staff will respect a child/young person's right to privacy.
- Children/young people's views, opinions and feelings will be heard and treated with respect.
- A culture will exist which allows children/young people to question decisions made about their care and, if felt to be treated unfairly, offered the right to complain (Complaints and Representation Policy).
- Risk assessments will be carried out for all children/young people.
- Staff will address bad practice by colleagues and ensure managers and senior managers are made aware.
- Incident reports will be completed following any incident involving restraint, disclosure, complaint, as laid out in our Incident Report Procedure.
- The head teacher will monitor the school's practice through incident reports, discussion with staff and children/young people and feedback from supervision.
- The procedure for child protection incidents will be followed at all times.

All staff members should be aware of *the need to be vigilant in detecting indicators of abuse.* This will be included in the training programme for teaching staff, and will be brought to the attention of every other staff member within the school.

Procedure guidelines

Child protection procedures will be considered under the following circumstances:

- An allegation of physical abuse by a current or former member of staff.
- An allegation of sexual abuse by a current or former member of staff.
- An allegation of bullying or emotional cruelty by a current or former member of staff.
- An allegation of intimidation by use of physical, emotional or sexual coercion by another child/young person.
- An allegation/disclosure of sexual activity between children/young people.
- An allegation or suspicion of a child/young person's involvement in prostitution.
- An allegation/disclosure of physical abuse by members of a child/young person's family or any previous carer.
- An allegation of bullying or emotional cruelty by members of a child/young person's family or any previous carer.
- Children/young people being at risk in other ways which may include allegations of physical or sexual abuse by members of the public. Allegations of manipulations through drugs or alcohol by members of the public.
- When a staff member is in receipt of information that may put children/young people at risk.

(Continued)

(Continued)

Disclosure of abuse

If a child/young person discloses abuse, whether current, ongoing, in the past, adults must not give a guarantee of confidentiality as this places the adult in an untenable position. However, the child/young person will need to feel they can trust the adult to handle the given information in their best interests.

The child/young person should be told what may happen next, but first and foremost the adult must listen sensitively to the child/young person.

You must never ask any leading questions. If you do, these can disqualify any further investigation by the police. If they did decide to proceed, you may be heavily cross-examined on the fact that you lead the child/young person. Adults should not ask for a detailed account as the child/young person may have to repeat the information later as part of an investigation.

A senior member of staff must be informed and a record of what said should be made by the end of that school day, as an incident report. It must not be written as a *statement* (this word must not be used). It should be headed:

'Report of discussion between ... [child/young person's name] and ... [adult's name] dates, time, venue and reference to any incident [with].'

Reporting abuse

All incidents that may need to be considered under the child protection procedures *must* be reported immediately to a senior member of staff. That member of staff will then consult with the Child Protection Coordinator. In the absence of this person, the Learning and Development Manager must be notified. These incidents will then be handed over to the Child Protection Coordinator on their return.

The following incidents come into this consideration:

- An allegation of physical, sexual or emotional abuse by a current member of staff.
- An allegation/disclosure of physical/sexual abuse by member(s) of a child/young person's family or any previous carers.
- Children/young people *being at risk* any other way.
- An allegation or suspicion of a child/young person's involvement in prostitution.

Following a verbal communication of the incident/disclosure/allegation to the Child Protection Coordinator, a written Incident Report must be completed immediately and given to the Child Protection Coordinator. This report should be word-processed as per the incident report procedure. In exceptional circumstances only, a legible handwritten copy can be accepted.

The Child Protection Coordinator will keep up-to-date information logged on a progress sheet.

The Child Protection Coordinator will then discuss with the head teacher the next steps that need to be taken.

These steps may include:

- requests made for further information from adults involved. These must not be written up as Incident Reports but as reports, which must be signed and dated by the author. These must be clearly written, bearing in mind that external agencies may need them and language and content must be clear. A distinction between adults and child/young people must be made and adults' titles must be given. Full names of adults involved must be included but full names of other children should not be given – only initials should be used.
- the school's Child Protection Coordinator being asked to see the injuries if there are any, record them, mark them on a body map, and access to a medical practitioner should be given where appropriate. The Child Protection Coordinator may seek consultation with Social Services at this stage.

The steps taken will be different for each category and the decision-making process and further action will need take the following into account:

1 An allegation of physical/sexual abuse by an adult in school

- Is the adult admitting the allegation? If so, they will be suspended.
- Is there clear evidence of physical/sexual abuse? If there is, the adult will be suspended immediately under the school's Disciplinary Procedure even if denying the allegation.
- Are there witnesses to support the allegation? If so, the adult will be suspended immediately.
- If there is no evidence, no acknowledgement and no immediate witness, or there are disputed perspectives, serious consideration must still be given to the nature of the allegation and the member of staff may still be suspended. There are, of course, times when children/young people 'complain' about an adult in the way they were held or treated. These 'complaints' will be viewed in context and may be processed under the Complaints Procedure.

Following consultation between the Child Protection Coordinator and the child/young person's parents, a decision will be made on whether to seek consultation with Social Services to gain clarification on the matter before proceeding further.

If a clear referral is the intended action, then an Initial Assessment and Referral for Children in Need to Social Services will need to be completed and faxed through to County Duty who in turn will pass it on to Social Services. An initial strategy discussion will take place between Social Services and the police. If it is decided to pursue the matter, Social Services will then contact the school to agree the way forward.

(Continued)

(Continued)

The issue of suspension is a highly sensitive one and must be seen as protection to both adult and child/young person while an investigation is made. It is important that it is understood that suspension is not to be seen in any prejudicial manner. For the child/young person, there will need to be work done by other staff members concerning the fear and anxieties about making an allegation. It is known that children/young people may make allegations out of anger or retribution, however, we must never reach this conclusion without careful consideration and discussion with other staff.

Whether or not the allegation is investigated by this process, it must still form part of the ongoing work with the child/young person as we need to understand 'why'.

If it is decided not to proceed any further after a consultation with Social Services, the member of staff will return to work as soon as possible. It may not be an immediate return to full-time duties until some facilitating work is done between the adult and child/young person.

However, if the decision is made that the school will need to proceed under Disciplinary Procedures, this will only take place once the Section 47 investigation has been concluded.

Ofsted will need to be informed at all stages – consultation, referral, suspension, disciplinary.

2 An allegation of physical/sexual activity between children/young people

- The major consideration is whether there is an imbalance or 'power' in the relationship between the two children/young people. This is to be discussed and decided by the head teacher in consultation with the Child Protection Coordinator.
- Does either child/young person 'feel' a victim to the other? Was their coercion either explicit or implicit?
- Following the NSPCC guidelines, a two year or more age difference between the children/young people will probably indicate an imbalance in the power relationship. Male/female imbalance of power needs to be considered, as well as the emotional age of the children/young people involved.

3 An allegation of physical/sexual abuse by members of a child/young person's family or previous carers

- Is this the first disclosure/allegation?
- What is the current contact between the child/young person and the family member or previous carers?

The Child Protection Coordinator, in liaison with local Social Services and family/carers, will decide how to proceed. The head teacher must be clear about the action that is to be taken.

4 Children/young people being at risk in any other ways which could include neglect, emotional abuse, etc. with leaver

- Is there the need for immediate action by a third party, i.e. the police?
- Have the parents/carers been informed?

The Child Protection Coordinator, in consultation with the local Social Services, will decide how to proceed. The head teacher must be clear about the action that is to be taken.

5 An allegation or suspicion of a child/young person's involvement in prostitution

- Is there a previous history of the child/young person engaging in this activity?

Following discussion with Social Services, it may be necessary to contact the local police to ensure the safety and welfare of the child/young person. The Child Protection Coordinator, in consultation with local Social Services and family/carers, will decide how to proceed.

Conduct throughout child protection referrals

All staff members involved with child protection procedures should bear in mind the interests of the child above all other considerations. Children who are designated Child in Need or who are placed on the child protection register should be known to all relevant staff members. Concerns relating to these children should be raised immediately with the Child Protection Coordinator. All records relating to child protection procedures should be kept securely and are confidential.

What is child abuse?

Child abuse is defined in the Department of Health's Safeguarding and Promoting the Welfare of Children Guidelines 2006 as:

1 **Neglect**
   Is the persistent failure to meet a child/young person's basic physical and/or psychological needs likely to result in the serious impairment of the child/young person's health or development? Neglect may occur during pregnancy as a result of maternal substance abuse. Once a child/young person is born, neglect may involve a parent or carer failing to provide adequate food and clothing, shelter (including exclusion from the home or abandonment), failing to protect a child/young person from physical and emotional harm or danger, failure to ensure adequate supervision (including the use of inadequate caretakers), failure to ensure access to appropriate medical care or treatment. It may also include neglect of, or unresponsiveness to, a child/young person's basic emotional needs.

2 **Physical abuse**
   This may involve hitting, shaking, throwing, poisoning, burning or scalding, drowning, suffocating or otherwise causing physical harm to a child/young person. Physical harm may also be caused when a parent or carer fabricates the symptoms or deliberately induces illness in a child/young person.

3 **Sexual abuse**
   This involves forcing or enticing a child/young person to take part in sexual activities, including prostitution, whether or not the child/young person is aware of what is happening. The activities may involve physical contact including penetrative (e.g. rape, buggery or oral sex) or non-penetrative acts. They may include non-contact activities such as involving children/ young people in looking at, or in the production of, pornographic material or watching sexual activities, or encouraging children/young people to behave in sexually inappropriate ways.

4 **Emotional abuse**
   Is the persistent ill treatment of a child/young person such as to cause severe and persistent adverse effects on the child/young person's emotional development? It may involve conveying to the child/young person that they are worthless or unloved, inadequate or valued only insofar as they meet the needs of another person. It may feature age or developmentally inappropriate expectations being imposed on children/young people. These may include interactions that are beyond the child/young person's developmental capability, as well as overprotection and limitation of exploration and learning, or preventing the child/ young person's participation in normal social interaction. It may involve seeing or hearing the ill treatment of another. It may involve serious bullying causing children/young people frequently to feel frightened or in danger, or the exploitation or corruption of children/young people. Some level of emotional abuse is involved in all types of maltreatment of a child/young person, though it may occur alone.

It can be extremely upsetting for school staff to discover that a child/young person may have been abused while at school or at home. It is easy to feel persecuted by the investigation, the impact of which on both adults and children/young people should not be underestimated. Adults and children/young people will need to be fully supported so that a climate of openness can be maintained in which it is felt to be safe to speak out. Even if the allegation is considered to be exaggerated or untrue, it is important that it should be taken seriously and the correct procedures followed. The person or authority to whom the allegations were made is enjoined in law to ascertain whether abuse has taken place. Social Services and the local Police Special Investigation Unit are jointly involved as investigating agencies.

Procedures for child protection referrals

The options for reporting abuse under child protection procedures based on Safeguarding and Promoting the Welfare of Children Guidance 2006 are two-fold:

Firstly, the Child Protection Coordinator can consult with a designated person at Social Services. This consultation is done over the telephone, the children/young people can be anonymous at this point and the consultation will seek to inform and help the Child Protection Coordinator in the decision of whether to make a formal referral or not. The consultation will be recorded, logged and given a reference number.

The second option is a full referral to County Duty. In order to do this, the Child Protection Coordinator will need the following:

1 An Initial Assessment and Referral form completed by the school.
2 A copy of the Incident Report.
3 Copies of the follow-up reports of discussions relevant to the understanding of the incident and investigation process.
4 The child/young person's details.
5 The opinion of the child/young person's family where appropriate.

The Child Protection Coordinator will then write a letter containing information on what action was taken immediately after the incident to protect the children/young people and a view of what further action might be taken. The parents, if appropriate, will be informed.

Attached to this letter will be the Incident Report and the child/young person's details – nothing more.

As stated earlier, if County Duty decide to proceed, they will inform Social Services who will contact the Child Protection Coordinator.

Following the initial strategy discussion, it may be necessary to arrange interviews with the child(ren)/young person(s). At this stage, the interviewers may ask for a pen picture of the child(ren)/young person(s) prior to interview.

The child/young person must be protected and their needs must be represented confidently to other professionals. It is more important to continue to protect the child/young person than to gain information to lead to prosecution.

Following any interview with the children/young people or staff by a social worker and police officer, a further strategy meeting will be held by Social

Services and attended by Social Services, police, parents and ourselves (the school's Child Protection Coordinator or deputy will attend).

The strategy meeting will decide how to proceed and what action is to be taken. There may be a number of these strategy meetings as the case is investigated. If the incident is serious, then a Child Protection Conference will be convened, as decided by the strategy meeting.

Strategies may be discussed over the telephone, outside of a meeting. Such strategies may be seeking a medical examination immediately with the local community paediatrician. A referral to the local community paediatrician can be made through the accident and emergency department at the local hospital. Written consent for the medical examination is preferable and this can only be provided by the person or department holding parental responsibility. However, if it is necessary to proceed with a medical examination in order to preserve evidence, this should be arranged following verbal consent which must be followed up in writing as soon as possible. The Child Protection Officer and head teacher must give careful consideration as to who is the most appropriate adult to accompany the child/young person. The paramount consideration is protecting the child/young person from further adult abuse, bearing in mind that bureaucratic actions or adult dynamics can easily perpetuate abuse.

The outcome of a strategy meeting will be recorded by the Child Protection Coordinator and action acted upon.

If the decision of the strategy meeting will be recorded by the Child Protection Conference, then this will be arranged as soon as possible. At all times, the school must facilitate speedy arrangements for strategy meetings and conferences. To bring all professionals together may take time, but we must hold on to the interest of the child/young person and as a principle not prolong the process. We must, therefore, prioritise such meetings if we are given dates without compromising the attendance of key people.

The Child Protection Conference

This will be convened by Social Services who are the investigating authority. They may also convene a conference to consider the wider implications of the alleged abuse, e.g. are other children/young people safe? In the case of child/young person to child/young person abuse, separate conferences will usually be held in respect of victim and abusers. The purpose of the conference is to assess the degree of risk, decide on the basis of this information, if registration is necessary and formulate an Interagency Child Protection Plan which will be implemented by a core group of professionals, including school personnel. Staff attending a Child Protection Conference for the first time will need to be prepared for the way in which such conferences are run and be clear as to what will be expected of them. This will be done by the Child Protection Coordinator.

Photocopiable:

Working with Parents © Carmel Digman and Sue Soan, 2008

Index